How The Steam Railways Came To
SURREY

Oliver Hayes

Bretwalda Books Ltd

First Published 2015
Text Copyright © Bretwalda Books 2015

Oliver Hayes asserts his moral rights to be recognised
as the author of this work.

Bretwalda Books,
Unit 8, Fir Tree Close, Epsom, Surrey KT17 3LD

info@BretwaldaBooks.com
www.BretwaldaBooks.com

ISBN 978-1-910440-29-2

Printed and bound in Great Britain by
Marston Book Services Ltd, Oxfordshire

Contents

Introduction

When I was a boy I lived on the north facing hill outside Esher that overlooks the main line from London to Portsmouth and Southampton. It had been built in 1838 by the London and Southampton Railway, later to become the famous London and South Western Railway (LSWR). From our front garden you could see the trains thundering back and forth along the embankment that ran like a stripe across the landscape. By then, of course, the glory days of steam in Surrey were long gone. It was electric trains that raced back and forth. But the odd steam train did go by, the plume of smoke drifting up into the air to disperse over the landscape.

Years later I was living down by the River Thames and commuting up to London by train from Surbiton along that self same LSWR mainline where I had grown up. Day after day I trudged up the hill to the striking inter-wars station to get on to one of the many commuter trains running up to Waterloo. By then all the steam trains had gone, but the mark of them was everywhere. The site of the water tower, the blackened undersides of the bridges and the engine sheds. I often wondered what Surrey had been like back in the days of steam.

My Uncle George had been a senior fireman on the LNER line running north from London. He used to tell me about his days on the footplate. He told me how he had started off as a teenager in the shed scrubbing and cleaning, gradually working his way up to be a fireman, first on shunters, then on local trains and finally on the great express trains that thundered along the main lines, belching smoke and steam as they powered up and down from London

Locomotive 30582 pulls out of Staines railway station toward the Staines West Curve. That curve of line was built in 1884 to allow trains to run direct from Woking to Windsor, but was abandoned in 1965 as rail use fell. The route of the line was subsequently built over.

to York, Newcastle and Edinburgh. But I think he had preferred the country lines with their quiet stations, bunnies hopping in the fields and old-style station masters.

Surrey had been like that once. The railways came to Surrey in the 1840s and they were still being built in the 1930s, making Surrey most unusual among the counties of England. Across most of the country, railway building had ground to a halt long before the line to Chessington was opened in 1939, complete with suitably modernistic station architecture. Moreover, Surrey suffered only one line closure in the Beeching years, leaving over 90% of its railway lines open and operating into the 21st century. Surrey is most fortunate from the railway point of view.

Those railways were to have dramatic impact on the landscapes, people and economy of Surrey. Indeed, the Surrey that we see today has been largely created by the railways. It is no exaggeration to say that more than any other county in England, Surrey has been built on railways.

This book sets out to describe How the Steam Railways came to Surrey. That age of steam in Surrey is remembered fondly by thousands. The fans of steam recall the many different locomotives that hurried along the lines, the travellers recall the grimy grit of smoke and steam filling carriages in summer when the windows were down, and all county residents look back on a less hurried time when the demands of a globalised world were still in the future and the good folk of Surrey could potter about their own business in their own way. I have spoken to dozens of them while researching this book. I am sorry that I missed the heyday of steam in Surrey, but glad that I did at least come in for the last few glimmers that reflected the glory days of long ago.

Since 1965 the county has lost the rough square shape that it had for most of its history. The northeastern corner of the county was in that year sliced off and handed over to London on the grounds that it had been covered by a vast suburban sprawl that belonged more to outer London than to Surrey. The county originally stretched along the south bank of the Thames to Southwark and Rotherhithe, but now stops before it reaches Croydon or Sutton. Even the County Hall, seat of the County Council, is outside of Surrey these days as it stands in Kingston upon Thames, now a London borough. This book deals with Surrey as it is now.

Chapter 1

Steam Comes to Surrey

B efore the steam railways come to the county of Surrey, it was neither a comfortable nor a prosperous place. Economic decline, depopulation, crime and social dislocation all stalked the county.

The area that had suffered most was the Weald, the low country to the south of the chalk downs. The local iron industry had lasted 2,000 years, relying on the local iron ore and on the forests that produced the charcoal needed by the smelting process. But then a method of using coal to smelt iron was found. The industry moved to areas with coal mines. By 1800 the Surrey iron industry was dead. Some people sold charcoal to London markets, while others exported timber. But neither really prospered due to the high transport costs.

The economy of the chalk hills of central Surrey was likewise in decline. This had been good sheep country for centuries, but from the 1820s onward imports of both wool and meat from the Americas and Australia undercut the price of the Surrey producers. The only bright spot was on Epsom Downs

A first day cover of stamps issued by the Post Office in 1994 to commemorate 150 years of railway history in Redhill. When the station was first opened in 1844 it was named Reigate as that was the nearest settlement of any size.

A Thames barge tied up to the wharf at Weybridge in the 19th century. Until the coming of the railways most heavy freight was carried on barges along rivers and canals. Goods unloaded from ocean-going ships at the London docks were transferred to barges such as this for onward transport inland. The coming of the railways was to change everything.

where horse racing was a growing activity. King James I had come here to test his horses in the early 17th century, and by the early 19th century classic races such the Derby and the Oaks were attracting crowds, as well as supporting a number of race horse businesses.

Epsom was also a minor health resort. A spring poured forth a salty water that had a laxative effect if drunk and soothed skin complaints if used in a bath. The wonder ingredient was later found to be a magnesium salt that has been commercially marketed as Epsom Salts.

The northeastern end of the county was covered by fertile alluvial soils laid down by the Rivers Thames, Mole and Wey. By the early 19th century the lands were producing fruit and vegetables for sale in the London markets. These were loaded on to carts and sent lumbering off over the roads toward the city, or loaded on to river barges and floated down.

Efforts had been made to solve the transport problems that had bedevilled Surrey for centuries. As early as the mid-17th century the Wey and Mole rivers were being widened, dredged and straightened to make them suitable for barge traffic that could carry goods up the Thames from the port of London.

The maintenance of roads and paths was a responsibility of the parish authorities. They tended to make the roads only as good as they needed to be for the locals to move their livestock about, haul wagons of hay or grain from field to farm and the like. In the early 18th century some major roads were taken over by private companies that charged a toll and used the money to pay for the road to be properly maintained. The Portsmouth Road was the first in Surrey to be made into a toll road, but others were to follow by the end of the century.

Meanwhile, a rival system of improving a road was being used elsewhere in places where heavy industrial loads were frequent. These would have been too heavy for the toll roads, tearing up the surface and rutting it. What these big, heavy wagons needed was a surface that was as hard as iron. So engineers began to make them out of iron. These iron roads were formed by fixing parallel pairs of iron tracks to the ground. The carts were then pulled along the tracks by horses or mules.

The construction of these iron railways was often hampered by the need to purchase land for the purpose. It thus became usual for an Act of Parliament to be passed that compelled the landowners to sell the necessary strips of land to the railway company in return for a fair market price. Debates in Parliament often revolved around which precise route should be taken, with both the rail companies and landowners using any influence they might have with MPs to try to get the route built as they wanted.

The station at Wanborough in 1910. The station was opened in 1891 on the Guildford to Alton line, which had been constructed in 1849. At this date it was still a quiet, isolated rural station but by the 1930s increased house building in the area had made it a busy commuter station.

The entrance to West Croydon Railway Station in about 1900. Note the variety of horse-drawn transport, both private and public. Once travellers had got to the railway station, they were still restricted to horse power to get about the local area.

In 1801 an Act of Parliament was passed to build an iron railway running from the River Thames at Wandsworth to the busy market town of Croydon. The Surrey Iron Railway company began construction work on the eight mile route at once. In 1803 a separate company, the Croydon, Merstham and Godstone Railway Company, was formed to build an extension to the line to stone quarries at Merstham and Godstone.

The new lines opened in 1805 and were an immediate success. The open-topped, four wheeled trucks carried all sorts of heavy loads, including building stone, bricks, grain and iron goods. Customers could either pay for a truckload to be hauled by the rail company, or they could pay a toll for their own horse and truck to use the railway.

The rails of the Surrey Iron Railway and the Croydon, Merstham and Godstone Railway were of the type known as plate rails. These consisted of rails with an L-shaped cross section. The wheels of the trucks ran on the horizontal section, which rested on the ground. The upright section of the rail was on the inside of the wheels and served to make sure that the wheels stayed on the rails. The system was perfectly adequate for wooden trucks being pulled at low speed by horses or mules.

The companies flourished. The new iron roads were able to function in all weathers and enabled a horse to pull a heavier load than it could on a conventional road. It seemed as if the future of transportation in Surrey was being settled. Routes used by humans would be developed by Turnpikes, long distance through routes for heavy goods would be by canal while shorter more local trade routes would be catered to by horse-drawn iron roads.

However, events were taking place many miles to the north that would disrupt these carefully laid plans. Within a few years all three of these promising methods of transport would be rendered obsolete, ineffective and bankrupt by a new invention. The steam railway was on its way.

While most of the people involved with the transport business had been concentrating on road surfaces — whether they were of stone or iron — one group of northern industrialists were rather more interested in motive power. It was this interest that was to bring the steam railways to Surrey.

It was the steam engine that was getting them excited. At first all steam engines were stationary and used to turn factory machinery or to pump water out of mines. As the technology of steam engines improved, they could be made smaller, lighter and more powerful. Finally, in 1804 a Cornish engineer named Richard Trevithick produced a steam engine that was small and light enough to mount on a truck. He linked the power output of the engine to the wheels of the truck and so produced a self-powered vehicle. In 1806 he sold a locomotive, complete with trucks and rails to a mine owner on Tyneside. The railway train, as it now became known, proved to be highly effective at hauling coal from the mine to a nearby dock to be loaded on to ships which then carried the coal to London for sale. Soon every mine owner wanted a steam railway to move his coal.

A delivery cart rumbles over a bridge just outside Weybridge in the 1890s. Even after the railways arrived most local transport was by horse and cart. Goods would be brought to a town or village by train, then transferred to a cart for transport to its final destination.

A Byway near Weybridge.

The Bournmouth Express enters Surbiton station as it emerges from the only big cutting on the LSWR route through Surrey in the 1930s. Kingston Council successfully blocked a route across the flat fields near their town and forced the railway to cut through the nearby St Mark's Hill.

Other engineers soon moved in to take up the task of building railways, the most famous of whom were the father and son team of George and Richard Stephenson. In 1825 the two completed the landmark Stockton and Darlington Railway. This nine mile long railway linked several coal mines to docks on the River Tees.

The Stockton and Darlington Railway introduced several technical innovations — including a purpose built passenger carriage that was hitched to the back of some coal trains to carry humans in some comfort. The gauge was of 4 feet 8 1/2 inches and the train wheels were flanged to run on I-section rails, as do all modern trains. The tracks were laid on a course as close to level as possible as Stephenson found his locomotive would run dangerously too fast on downhill slopes, and would struggle to get up hills.

The advantages of a steam railway over canals and roads were immediately obvious. Steam trains could go much faster — speeds of 30 mph were common — and the high speeds could be maintained over long distances. The railways could carry heavier loads than any cart, and by 1830 had a carrying capacity equal to that of canal and river barges. Moreover, the operating costs in terms of how much it cost to move a ton of goods over a given distance were low compared to those of carts and barges.

The only drawback to the new transportation system was that the costs of building the line in the first place were enormous. Anyone paying out for the building of a railway had to be very confident that there would be enough demand for transportation along the route to turn a profit and repay the construction costs. It was for this reason that most early railways were built to carry freight. It was relatively easy to predict how much coal a mine might produce to be moved to a nearby dock.

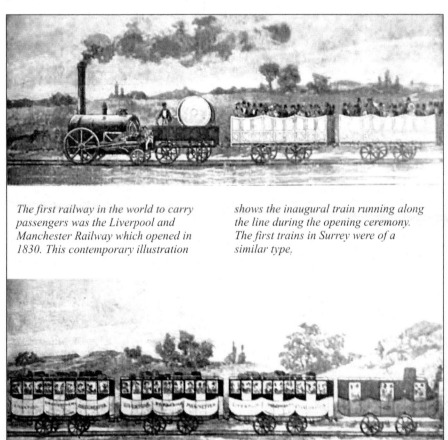

The first railway in the world to carry passengers was the Liverpool and Manchester Railway which opened in 1830. This contemporary illustration shows the inaugural train running along the line during the opening ceremony. The first trains in Surrey were of a similar type.

Building the Main Lines

The first steam railway to be built in Surrey was primarily a goods line which opened in 1839. This was the London and Croydon Railway, which ran from what is now London Bridge station to what is now West Croydon. This line is now entirely within Greater London.

Much more difficult was the task of anticipating how many passengers might want to travel a particular route. Despite this it was a line built with passengers in mind that was the first to strike out across Surrey on a route from London to Brighton. The fact that part of the route ran through Surrey was merely coincidental.

The idea was first suggested in 1825 when a group of businessmen formed a company called, rather optimistically, The Surrey, Sussex, Hampshire, Wiltshire and Somerset Railway. They employed the famous bridge architect John Rennie to survey what they intended to be the first route of an extensive

network, that ran from London to Brighton. No sooner had he begun work than the plan was dropped. Four years later Rennie was hired again, this time to survey two different routes. The first was to take in the intermediate towns of Dorking, Horsham and Shoreham, while the second was to run direct between

John Rennie was an experienced builder of bridges when he was hired in 1829 to survey a route across Surrey for a railway linking London to the south coast. He was later employed in Sweden and Portugal surveying and laying out railways in those countries.

London and Brighton. This time he completed his work, but the company foundered due to a lack of funds and interest.

In 1835 the London and Brighton Railway (L&BR) was founded and bought up Rennie's work. This new company favoured the direct route, but the matter had to go before a Parliamentary committee, which took months to pore over the various options before finally deciding that the L&BR had been right all along. Rennie's direct route was therefore adopted, even though it would involve the building of several expensive tunnels and bridges that could have been avoided on the longer route.

As with the earlier horse-drawn iron roads, the new railways required an Act of Parliament to compel landowners to sell, gain the right for the railway to cross rivers and other legal matters. The L&BR act was passed by Parliament in July 1837, but the MPs had introduced some variations. The railway was not to have its own London station, but to use that of the already existing London and Croydon Railway. The line would begin at Norwood and then follow the Rennie direct route, with branch lines authorised to Lewes and Shoreham.

A train approaches Milford in about 1904. Among the railway staff awaiting the train on the far platform is a ticket collector and a porter with his trolley. Even a relatively quiet station such as this would have had a number of full time staff on duty to care for the needs of the travelling public.

The LSWR Waterloo-Bournemouth express passes through Surbiton hauled by 4-6-0 locomotive No.443. The sudden emergence of relatively cheap long distance travel had a profound effect on society in Surrey.

The MPs also introduced an amendment that the L&BR had opposed. The Members of Parliament were at the same time considering a proposal to link London to Dover and Folkestone put forward by the South Eastern Railway (SER). For some reason the parliamentarians felt that there would not be enough trains coming into London to justify the bother of having two lines. They therefore stipulated that the SER and L&BR should share a line from Norwood south through the North Downs. The two railway companies would have their own lines only after that.

In the House of Lords, the railway found itself confronted by the influential Lord Monson. Monson had nothing against railways, in fact he was generally in favour of them. However, the proposed route would run very close to his home at Gatton Hall, southwest of Merstham. The house stood on a south facing slope looking across a shallow valley in which had been constructed an artificial lake to improve the view. And the railway route would be on the far side of the lake and in full view of the house. In order to mollify any objections that Lord Monson might have to this, the railway placed Merstham Station immediately outside the gates of Gatton Hall on Battlebridge Lane, almost a mile away from Merstham itself. The villagers were able to watch the trains passing within 50 yards of their homes, but had to face a lengthy walk to get on the things.

Such considerations would bedevil the building of the railways across Surrey and lead to some decidedly odd situations. At least in Merstham's case the situation was later sorted out when the station was moved to its present location in the village centre.

Despite these problems, construction began in 1838 under the guidance of engineer John Urpeth Rastrick. At the height of the works, in the summer of 1840, Rastrick had 6,206 men, 962 horses, five locomotives and seven stationary engines under his control. The building of this line was Surrey's first introduction to railway building, railwaymen and to railways in general. It was not an altogether happy experience. Because of the need to keep the track as level as possible, the route through the North Downs called for a deal of major engineering works. The most important of these was the tunnel between Coulsdon and Merstham. The tunnel was 1 mile 253 yards long, with

Left: In the course of its history the London, Brighton and South Coast Railway had some impressive figures among its senior management. Among these was Sir Walter Barttelot, 1st Baronet CB, PC. He came from an ancient Sussex family and was an extensive landowner who also served as MP for Horsham.

Be;ow: A ticket for a journey from Haslemere to Guildford. Such relatively short distance journeys were common on the steam railways of Surrey, linking as they did assorted towns and villages.

An undated photograph, though probably from the 1920s, shows a Gladstone class locomotive hauling a passenger train into East Croydon. Commuting to London is now taken for granted but at this date was still a relatively new phenomenon.

an extensive cutting over 100 feet deep leading into its northern end. The chalk excavated from the cutting and tunnel were used to build embankments that served to flatten out the slope up to the tunnel entrance.

The tunnelling through the Downs was hampered by the fact that the hills were pocked by old mine workings. One of these old tunnels had filled up with water and when the railway workers broke through a flood followed. One man was killed and large quantities of equipment destroyed.

The building work meant that, for the first time, Surrey was the temporary home to large numbers of navvies — 6,000 of them in all. These navvies, or workmen, were a distinguishing feature of the railway construction period. Without them there could have been no railways, yet they were a constant source of trouble and frustration. The word "navvy" is derived from "navigators" and referred to the days when gangs of workmen moved about the country building canals, or inland navigation waterways. At this date there were no mechanical diggers, bulldozers or trucks. Everything had to be done by hand or by horse power. The navvies were equipped with picks and shovels to do the digging, and had horse-drawn carts to haul the rubble away from the

A train calls at Boxhill and West Humble Station in 2009. This was originally built as a prestige station with a riot of coloured tiles and glazed bricks. The colours have since faded and the station is now mostly unmanned, but it remains an architectural gem.

site. The amount of muscle power needed to dig a cutting 100 feet deep through solid chalk was enormous, which was why so many men were employed on this and other railway projects.

By the nature of the job, the men moved about constantly. As each rail line progressed they moved along with it, in the case of the LB&SCR/SER line they started just outside London and moved slowly south over the passing months. And when one railway line was finished they had to move right across the country to start work on the next one. They lived in temporary wooden shacks, little more than sheds that were dismantled and moved on as the worksite moved. It was no life for a family man, so nearly all navvies were unmarried young men who came to work the railways for a few years to earn money before returning home to settle down, or finding some less physically arduous job. At this date, most navvies were Englishmen with the majority coming from economically depressed areas — such as Surrey.

Inevitably, with huge numbers of young men encamped together things could sometimes turn a bit rough. The most reliably difficult day was Saturday, when the men were paid. Thirsts were great among the navvies and huge quantities of beer could be consumed. This led to frayed tempers, imagined slights and frequent recourse to fisticuffs among the men. When efforts were made to limit the amount of beer available on a Saturday evening a strike followed.

One of the most distinguished managers of the LB&SCR was Edward Ponsonby, Earl of Bessborough. He was a director from 1895, taking over as Chairman in 1908 and holding that post until his death in 1920.

The Railway Tavern near the top of Sutton High Street photographed in 1885. At this date Sutton was a prosperous rural market town. However the changes brought about by the railway that would transform it into a suburb of south London were already beginning.

Generally the works in Surrey passed off without any serious incident — largely due to the fact that the route did not pass through any major towns. The navvies were not, therefore, tempted to pour into a town to drink the pubs dry and get into altercations with locals as happened elsewhere.

In an attempt to curb disputes with locals, the railway building contractors took to providing everything the men would want. This process was still in its infancy as the LB&SCR/SER lines were built, but would later give rise to some highly sophisticated organisations. The company provided cookhouses where three meals a day were served. These meals were paid for with tokens which the navvies were given in place of some of their cash wages. The navvies could also arrange for part of their pay to be held back and either sent to their families or invested in a bank. The idea was to encourage the men to use their wages wisely, saving for the future or helping their kith and kin instead of spending it all in the local pub.

As events fell out, the branch line from Brighton to Shoreham was completed first, in May 1840. This short section ran as an isolated little line for some months before it was linked to London. The main line was opened

The village of Woking as it appeared in the early days of the railway. The village stood several miles from the station and is now *known as Old Woking to differentiate it from the new town that sprang up around the railway station in the later 19th century.*

in two sections: the Norwood Junction to Haywards Heath section, which included the Surrey section, was opened on 12 July 1841 and the Haywards Heath to Brighton section the following September. A special inaugural train for the company directors and investors left Brighton at 8.45am on 21 September and arrived in London one hour and 45 minutes later. Nobody had ever travelled between the two towns so quickly before. The branch line to Lewes was not to be completed until 1846.

Because the line was intended for passengers, not freight, efforts were made to make it rather more attractive than was normal. The noted architect David Mocatta was hired to embellish the stations, bridges and tunnel entrances. He opted for an Italianate style that drew its inspiration from Renaissance Florence. Some of his work remains at Brighton, but at other stations it has been swept away in subsequent rebuildings.

There were, at this time, a large number or railway companies each operating their own individual lines. It was not long before the directors of the companies realised that they could save money, and therefore boost profits, if the companies shared locomotives, rolling stock, personnel and stations. In some cases the companies pooled resources but remained separate, but in the case of the L&BR the directors opted for a merger. On 27 July 1846, the

L&BR merged with the London and Croydon Railway, the Brighton and Chichester Railway and the Brighton, Lewes and Hastings Railway to form the London, Brighton and South Coast Railway (LB&SCR). Operating profits rose accordingly.

Meanwhile the shared line through the North Downs had been causing friction between the L&BR and the SER. The joint line ended at an empty field a couple of miles east of Reigate. Thereafter the L&BR line ran south to Horley and then out of the county into Sussex. The SER line headed east through Godstone toward Tonbridge and thence to the Channel ports. At the junction the L&BR built a station that they named Reigate. Passengers who were hoping actually to go to Reigate were faced with a fair walk from the station to the town. Such a situation was unfortunate, but had been dictated by the geology of the route. What was slightly ridiculous was that the SER built a completely separate station a few hundred yards away. Not wanting to give it the same name as the L&BR station, the SER chose to name it after a nearby landmark: Redstone Hill. The increasingly acrimonious disputes about who could run which train when over the shared line were inherited by the LB&SCR.

The Bournemouth Express enters Surbiton station as it emerges from the only big cutting on the LSWR route through Surrey in the 1930s. Kingston Council successfully blocked a route across the flat fields near their town and forced the railway to cut through the nearby St Mark's Hill.

Station Road, Redhill.

Station Road, Redhill, in 1912. The grand Victorian and Edwardian shops and buildings show how far Redhill had come since 1841 when the station, then named "Reigate" had opened in an empty field miles from the nearest buildings.

The various delays constructing the line to Brighton meant that, in fact, the first passenger railway to open in Surrey was actually the London and Southampton Railway (LSR) line which opened partially in 1838 and completely on 11 May 1840. Unlike the L&BR, the LSR was originally envisaged as a freight line. The line was supported by the merchants and town council of Southampton. During the recent Napoleonic Wars they had seen many ships sailing up the Channel to London being attacked and sometimes captured by French raiding ships. They believed that they could make Southampton more attractive to sea captains if the port offered a safe method of moving goods from the docks there to London. At first they contemplated a canal link to the upper Thames, but in 1830 they turned to the railways.

The idea was first put forward by Abel Ros Dottin, the MP for Southampton. He put together a group of rich men who paid for a formal prospectus which was put before a packed public meeting in Southampton in February 1831. The meeting resulted in the founding of the Southampton, London and Branch Railway and Dock Company. The line was to run from Southampton Docks to a site at Nine Elms, upstream of London, where docks were to built. Goods were to be unloaded from ocean going ships at Southampton, taken by rail to Nine Elms and then transferred to canal barges for onward shipment down the Thames to London or up the canal network to the Midlands and North. The company hired engineer Francis Giles who surveyed a route from Southampton by way of Winchester, Woking Common and Kingston to Nine Elms. By this time the directors had changed the company name to the rather snappier London and Southampton Railway (LSR). The Act of Parliament authorising land acquisition and the like was passed on 25 July 1834.

Construction began under Giles immediately, but he proved to be unsatisfactory to one influential shareholder and was replaced by Joseph Locke. As with many early railways, the new line was opened in stages. Nine Elms to Woking Common opened on 21 May 1838, thus beating the L&BR to opening the first steam railway in Surrey. The second section, from Woking Common west out of Surrey, opened in September 1838 and by May 1840 the line had reached Southampton Docks. By this date the company had changed its name again to become the London and South Western Railway Company (LSWR). This railway company proved to be highly successful and soon extended its lines far beyond Southampton.

The LSWR avoided the need for expensive and time consuming engineering works by skirting north of the chalk Downs all the way to Hampshire and then taking advantage of a natural break in the hills to turn south to the coast. The only big cutting necessary came when the town council of Kingston refused the line permission to cross their lands for fear that the railway might harm the

Joseph Locke was the chief engineer of the LSR during the years that the first lines were pushed through Surrey. He had been trained under the Stephensons and went on to become of the greatest civil engineers of his age, working on projects across Britain and France. What is now Britain's West Coast Main Line is largely Locke's work.

prosperous horse fair in the town. The wrangle with Kingston Council lasted months and consumed much Parliamentary time. In the end, the company agreed to divert the line south in order to get the Act passed. The railway built a station named Kingston upon Rail at the nearest spot to the town for those wishing to visit. Some years later a branch line was built to Kingston and so Kingston upon Rail took the name of a nearby hamlet: Surbiton.

I should tell you that for some years in the 1990s I served as a councillor representing Surbiton. By then Surbiton and Kingston town councils had merged into one. Those of us from Surbiton used to greatly enjoy teasing the Kingston councillors (who greatly outnumbered us) whenever the subject of transport came up for debate. The shortsightedness of the Kingston Town Council in having turned away the railway was always brought up as a reason why we Subiton councillors should be listened to. It never worked out that way, of course, the Kingston councillors insisted on having their way. Go to Kingston these days by car, bus or train and see what they have made of it. But I digress.

The directors of the LSWR proved to be rather inept at the naming of stations. The first stop west of Kingston on Rail was called Ditton Marsh. It did, indeed, stand on the edge of that boggy marsh but the later name of Esher, after the nearest village, was rather more appealing. Further down the line a station named Woking Heath was built utterly isolated on the sandy upland of that name, about a mile and a half from the village of Woking. It was two years before somebody built a hotel next to the station.

The directors of the LSWR soon noticed something rather odd. All sorts of people from Surrey were getting on their trains at the little local stations to go up to London. It had been thought that these stops would be used primarily for dropping off freight that would then be distributed to the local area by horse and cart. But passengers were starting to take over from freight. Some went on business, others for pleasure, but they were travelling in ever increasing numbers. Extra carriages had to be bought and hitched up and soon passenger-only trains were running. But there was one great source of complaint. The

A luggage label for a piece of luggage being transported to Godalming by the LSWR. When the railways began to be built it was mostly for the purpose of transporting freight, with passenger traffic becoming important later on.

Woking Station.

Woking station in 1906. By this date what had begun as a station set amid empty heathland had become the focus for a large town. The building of huge numbers of houses around the station had encouraged a massive growth in commuting to London and in the population of Woking.

terminus at Nine Elms meant that the London bound travellers had to walk or take a horse-drawn bus to get into central London.

In 1844 the LSWR went back to Parliament to ask for a new Act that would enable them to push their lines right into the heart of the metropolis. The resulting Act of July 1845 authorised a line from Nine Elms to London Bridge, with intermediate stations at Vauxhall and Waterloo Bridge. The company raised £950,000 and began construction. By 1848 the line had reached Waterloo Bridge and the station there — and the one at Vauxhall — was opened on 11 July. The engineering works had cost rather more than expected, so the LSWR directors called a temporary halt to construction. The rest of the line to London Bridge, they decided, could be finished off later.

In the event, of course, the rest of the line never was finished. The terminal has remained at Waterloo Bridge, later renamed just Waterloo, to the present day. For many years, however, the station layout was that of a through station with tracks running on past the platforms. As a result the ever expanding station with its additional lines and platforms came to acquire a notoriously complicated layout. As each new platform was added it was given a new number or name that bore no logical link to the ones next to it. Some were even on a different level to the main platforms.

The confusion that passengers encountered at this old Waterloo station were humorously described by the writer Jerome K. Jerome in his classic book "Three Men in a Boat". Along with a friend Jerome describes how he tried to catch a train to Kingston from Waterloo.

"We got to Waterloo at eleven, and asked where the eleven-five started from. Of course nobody knew; nobody at Waterloo ever does know where a train is going to start from, or where a train when it does start is going to, or anything about it. The porter who took our things thought it would go from number two platform, while another porter, with whom he discussed the question, had heard a rumour that it would go from number one. The station-master, on the other hand, was convinced it would start from the local.

"To put an end to the matter, we went upstairs, and asked the traffic superintendent, and he told us that he had just met a man who said he had seen it at number three platform. We went to number three platform, but the authorities there said that they rather thought that train was the Southampton express, or else the Windsor loop. But they were sure it wasn't the Kingston train, though why they were sure it wasn't they couldn't say.

"Then our porter said he thought that must be it on the high-level platform; said he thought he knew the train. So we went to the high-level platform, and saw the engine-driver, and asked him if he was going to Kingston. He said he

Surbiton Station as it was before the First World War. The station buildings were demolished in the 1920s and a new station built, while the railings were taken away in 1940 to assist the war effort. Only the small roundabout remains to this day.

Selhurst Station in 1908. Note the member of staff with his back to the camera watching the steam engine pulling into the platform. The members of the public on the platform seem more interested in the photographer. In 1912 this station would be rebuilt with quadruple lines.

couldn't say for certain of course, but that he rather thought he was. Anyhow, if he wasn't the 11.5 for Kingston, he said he was pretty confident he was the 9.32 for Virginia Water, or the 10 a.m. express for the Isle of Wight, or somewhere in that direction, and we should all know when we got there. We slipped half-a-crown into his hand, and begged him to be the 11.5 for Kingston.

"'Nobody will ever know, on this line,' we said, 'what you are, or where you're going. You know the way, you slip off quietly and go to Kingston.'

"'Well, I don't know, gents,' replied the noble fellow, 'but I suppose some train's got to go to Kingston; and I'll do it. Gimme the half-crown.'

"Thus we got to Kingston by the London and South-Western Railway.

"We learnt, afterwards, that the train we had come by was really the Exeter mail, and that they had spent hours at Waterloo, looking for it, and nobody knew what had become of it."

Not until a general rebuilding in the 20th century did Waterloo gain its modern form with parallel platforms numbered consecutively.

Meanwhile the SER was progressing with its line from Redstone Hill to the Channel ports. The SER expected that their main business profits would come from goods and passengers heading from London to the ports. Not much traffic was expected from stations along the way. For this reason only one station was built in Surrey: Godstone. As so often, this was something of a misnomer for the station was located 3 miles from the village in the midst of Wealden woodland. As at Woking a hotel was added some years later, though at Godstone it was more by way of a small pub with a couple of rooms.

West of Godstone, the navvies had to build a tunnel through Pound Hill. The tunnel was to be 1,326 yards long, but construction proved to be difficult. Pound Hill was composed of heavy clays interspersed by sandstone boulders and fragmented layers. The work took far longer than expected, so that the navvies' camp at Seven Acre Wood began to take on some of the attributes of a permanent village. After the work was completed in 1844, the chief engineer, Frederick Walter Simms, wrote a book based on his experiences that he called Practical Tunnelling. The volume became one of the standard reference works for civil engineers and remained continuously in print until 1896.

Back at Reigate, the two railway companies managed to reach an agreement in April 1844 and built a new, joint station to replace their individual stops. By this time a village had sprung up around the railway junction, it was to continue to grow over the coming years and would eventually become a sizeable town.

The economic benefits of having a rail link to the outside world were by this date becoming obvious. Railways could prosper not only by taking over

By the time this photograph was taken in 1962 at Oxted, the age of steam was drawing rapidly to a close. Locomotive 31324 takes on water as it prepares to leave heading into London.

freight and passenger traffic that had previously gone by road or barge, but could actually create traffic for themselves simply by offering a fast, cheap and convenient service. If Woking Common and Godstone stations remained in rural isolation for some years, others did not. The station then known as Reigate was rapidly acquiring a settlement. It began to occur to town councils, landowners and businessmen that they could expect to reap rich profits from a local railway.

In Surrey the first people to wake up to this fact were a group of businessmen in Guildford. They got the support of the town council for a railway line to run from their town to the LSWR station at Woking Heath. Accordingly the Guildford Junction Company (GJC) was formed and moves began to have an Act of Parliament passed. Obviously there would need to be co-operation with the LSWR.

The GJC opened talks with the LSWR with a view to having a platform at Woking Heath dedicated to the GJC line. In the event, the LSWR went much further. The company studied the proposal and recognised the potential profits that might be had from a line to Guildford, and already foresaw that the route could be pushed through the gap in the Downs at Guildford into the lands beyond. They therefore offered to buy out the original investors in the GJC, build the railway and operate it. The business community in Guildford was delighted. They were going to get their railway without needing to go to all the bother of building it or running it. They signed without delay. The line to Guildford opened on 5 May 1845. It proved to be such a success that it was upgraded to a double line in 1847. Two years later the line was pushed on to Godalming. In 1859 the LSWR continued the line through Godalming to Haslemere and so to Portsmouth. The line was thus upgraded to being a major through route with more frequent trains than had been envisaged.

What had happened at Guildford caused something of a sensation. It was now clear that a group of private citizens or a town council could promote a railway venture of interest to themselves in the hope that if they were able to demonstrate the financial viability of the scheme it would be bought up and constructed by a larger company.

It would not be long before dozens of different railway schemes were being promoted by all manner of individuals and organisations who had no real desire to build or run the railway themselves, but were keen to get an existing railway company interested. Most of these schemes resulted in branch lines over only short routes aimed at linking a specific town to the main rail network.

One such scheme in Surrey that proved successful was the Thames Valley Railway. This was formed by W.S. Lindsay, lord of the manor of Shepperton, to link that village to the main rail network. Lindsay was quite open about his intentions not to operate the railway himself but to interest another company in doing so. Shepperton lay north of the LSWR line to Southampton and south of the Great Western Railway (GWR) line through Staines to Reading. Lindsay tried the GWR first, but he found their terms for running the line to be unacceptable, so he turned to the LSWR. They offered more generous terms, but on condition that the new line linked to their main line at Twickenham. Lindsay agreed and the Shepperton branch line opened on 1 November 1864, being dualled in 1878.

Rather less successful, at least at first, was the Caterham Railway Company. In this instance the independent company, backed by local landowners and business interests, actually built the rail line that ran from its terminal at Caterham along the narrow, steeply-sided valley in the Downs to link to the LB&SCR at what is now Purley. The line opened in 1856, but was not a financial success, and the LB&SCR was not interested in buying it. In 1859 the SER offered to take the loss-making railway off the hands of the promoters. The sum paid was barely half what it had cost to build the railway in the first place. The SER, with more experience of running railways, introduced new working practices and managed to scrape a profit. The line would later become more profitable, but for reasons unforeseen in the 1850s.

Meanwhile the large rail companies were pushing ahead with schemes of their own. The most significant of these was the LB&SCR with what was to become known as the Mid-Sussex Line. This began as a line from Croydon to Epsom, opened in May 1847. The LSWR then built a line to Epsom from Wimbledon, opening a second station in the town. This encouraged a consortium from Leatherhead to form the Epsom and Leatherhead Railway in 1856 with a view to persuading one of the larger companies to build an extension stretching the 4 miles to Leatherhead. The company built a single-track line, which opened in 1859 and then quickly sold out to the LSWR. Six years later the LSWR and LB&SCR signed an agreement under which the line to Leatherhead was jointly owned and trains from both networks could use the rails.

Meanwhile, the LSWR announced plans to build a line west from Leatherhead to Guildford, a scheme that would be completed in 1885. The same men who had first raised the idea of a line from Epsom to Leatherhead now began promoting a line from that town to Dorking. The LB&SCR took

The Prospectus for the Horsham, Dorking and Leatherhead Railway as published in The Times on 5 November 1862. This private company was formed to promote the idea for a route and to demonstrate its economic viability. Once this was achieved, the company sold out to the more established LB&SCR which began work on the new line in 1867.

up the idea and began work in 1867.

The only feasible route for a railway from Leatherhead to Dorking was along the Mole Valley, across land that was owned by Thomas Grissell. Grissell was not only a vastly wealthy businessman but was also the owner of a large construction company that, among other things, was building railway lines elsewhere in the country. Grissell announced that as part of the price for selling his land he wanted to have a railway station built close to his grand house at Norbury Park. Not only that, but he wanted it built to his own designs. The result was the magnificent West Humble station, now Box Hill and West Humble. Now a listed building, the station is a riot of neo-Gothic arches, coloured tiles and patterned brickwork on a truly astonishing scale for what was and remains a little used halt.

Having thus got through the barrier of the North Downs, the LB&SCR decided to extend the line to Horsham, which they did in 1867, and on to other towns in Sussex. This Mid-Sussex Line followed a winding route that no sensible company would have followed if the ambition from the first had been to link Horsham to London, but which had resulted from the piecemeal way in which it was developed.

The completion of this line brought to an end the first rush of railway building across Surrey. The county was now crossed by main lines heading from London to Brighton, Southampton, Portsmouth and Horsham. There would be much later construction work for various reasons, but the initial boom was over.

33

Chapter 3

The Surrey Industrial Boom

The arrival of the railways made it possible to travel further, faster and cheaper than ever before. This in itself was to have profound consequences for Surrey and the people who lived there, as we shall see, but it was the ability to transport goods and products that had the most immediate and obvious impact on the county. Surrey rapidly experienced a boom in prosperity made possible by the railway.

Dorking was one of the first towns to find that its local industry received a boom from the coming of steam. Since at least the Tudor period, Dorking had been known as the home of a particular type of domestic fowl, the Dorking Hen. This bird was, and is, pure white in colour with a long body and short legs compared to other breeds.

The good folk of Dorking and surrounding villages had long made it their business to produce eggs, for the Dorking Hen is a prolific layer. These eggs were packed in straw, then loaded on to carts and taken north to London where they were sold. When the railway came it was suddenly possible to send eggs to market so fast that they could be served on a London table the same day that they were laid in Dorking. The numbers of eggs leaving Dorking daily increased dramatically.

Moreover, the speed and smoothness of the journey made it worth sending to market not only eggs, but young birds as well. Before the trains came, poulterers in Dorking sent most eggs to market and kept only as many birds as they needed for the laying flock. Now they could profitably keep some birds until they were adult, then send them to market as young fowl suitable for roasting. There was for a while in London a heated dispute as to whether town-bred or country-bred birds were of better eating quality, but it was not long before the public came to prefer the country-bred fowl. Dorking's poulterers had a new business, and it was booming. The importance of the fowl trade to Dorking is now commemorated by a 20 foot tall metal statue of a Dorking Hen on a roundabout at the junction of the A24 and A25 just east of the town centre. The trade has since declined as mass production of battery chickens in other counties came to dominate the business in the later 20th century.

Dorking was not alone in enjoying a railway-driven business boom. The Tillingbourne stream rises on Leith Hill, then flows northwest through Abinger and Gomshall to Shere and Chilworth after which it empties into the Wey at Shalford. The stretch around Gomshall flows over a sandy bed, which makes this pure water ideal for the growing of watercress. The local farmers had known this for centuries, and had always grown small quantities for local consumption. But then the railway line from Guildford to Reigate opened on 15 October 1849, with a station at Gomshall.

The local farmers noticed, and dammed the Tillingbourne at intervals to produce wide, shallow beds in which watercress could be produced. Several of these remain to this day. In the days before domestic fridges had been invented, watercress had to be fresh to be worth eating. The Gomshall growers became adept at sending their workers out into the wet fields at dawn to pick

Betchworth in the 1930s, a time of change for the station. This stop had previously been the site of two signal boxes, while the station was manned by three permanent staff. However technical improvements did away with the need for the boxes.

As well as the railways open to the public, Surrey also boasted a number of entirely private steam railways that were used by quarries, factories and other industrial concerns. This narrow gauge railway is on the Costam Factory estate at Croydon in 1925.

the cress, having it divided into bunches and set into wooden crates, then sent off to be on sale in London markets by lunchtime.

By 1880 the village was sending some 400 tons of watercress up to London by rail every year. The scale of the trade then remained fairly constant, climbing to around 450 tons by 1939. The Second World War and the upheavals its caused effectively ended the trade and the exports by steam railway. This did not come as so much of a blow to the railways as might be expected. Watercress is a bulky, but low weight freight. The wooden boxes took up a large amount of room both on stations and in wagons, yet the railways charged for freight by weight. Moving watercress was less profitable for the railway companies than almost any other type of industrial or agricultural produce.

Both the Dorking Hens and the Gomshall watercress businesses were located in the Weald, south of the chalky uplands, but the sandy heaths north of the chalk benefited as well. The thin acidic soils were not much good for conventional farming, but they were favourable to the raising of ornamental shrubs that preferred well-drained, light soils. Several nurseries had sprung up in the area to grow such shrubs for the gentry interested in gardening — but it had always been a small scale, specialised business. The age of steam changed that in two dramatic ways. First the building of a railway through the area in the 1850s, expanded with branch lines in the 1860s and 1870s, meant that any shrubs grown in the area could be shipped out speedily to their destination. This meant that the plants were out of the natural soil and in tubs for a much shorter period of time than had ever been possible in the days of cart and canal. The shrubs were much more likely to survive long journeys in a fit condition to take well in their new homes.

Perhaps more important was the fact that railways made it possible for people to live some miles from where they worked, and thus the concept of the suburb was born. For the first time even quite humble city folk had a small garden. And they wanted ornamental plants to grow in them. Business boomed and by 1870 around two tons of plants in pots were leaving the area by rail every day.

It was not only agricultural businesses that benefited from the coming of steam. Although the central hills of Surrey are predominantly chalk, there are sections composed of Upper Greensand, a form of sandstone that is easily worked and highly resistant to heat. It was, therefore, ideal for use as domestic hearthstones. Given that every home in England was heated by open fires until well into the 20th century, the demand for hearthstones was huge. The very first rails laid in Surrey, those of the horse drawn Surrey Iron Railway, had been built to access the quarries at Merstham and Godstone. When steam trains

Holmwood Station in the 1930s, when the main business here was freight related to the adjacent Schermuly Pistol Rocket Works.

The station was opened in May 1867 but has never been a large structure.

came, the rate of production boomed as well. When gas and electricity began to replace open fires as a form of domestic heating the business declined and had vanished by 1960.

Some businesses were so dependent on the steam trains that they had their own branch lines. Such a one was the chalk extraction works at Betchworth, owned by the Dorking Lime Co. In 1866 a branch was built by the SER from behind the north platform at Betchworth Station to run to the works where it joined the privately run, standard gauge network of tracks within the works themselves. The extensive works not only quarried chalk, but also burnt it into lime — a product useful in all sorts of industrial processes. Rather surprisingly these internal railways, complete with their six steam engines, continued in use until 1960 when motorised trucks took over the tasks. They were, therefore, the last steam engines to be in regular employment in the county.

Another, though smaller, chalk and lime works was also so busy as to deserve its own branch line. This was the Brockham Brick, Stone and Coal Co works at Brockham. The SER opened a side line in 1866. The works also had an internal rail network, though here it was a 2ft gauge light railway. The works closed in 1936. Two other chalk and lime works operated at Merstham and Oxted, both of which had private lines linking them to the public rail network. All of them boomed as a direct result of the age of steam arriving in the county.

The damp, low lying Weald concealed in places a clay substrata that was ideal for making bricks. These had not been much exploited before the age of steam for the simple reason that bricks are heavy to transport, and so could not be taken far over the poor roads of the area. The coming of the railways changed everything and soon there were several booming brickworks in the county. The Sussex Brick Co. opened a large works north of Lingfield which had two private sidings off the Oxted to East Grinstead line. The railway not

A label issued by Southern Railway to be attached to a pack of used tickets collected at a station for forwarding to the office at Dorking North. The used tickets were then processed not only to correlate with tickets sold, but also to work out how much of a journey had taken place on board Southern trains and how much on trains belonging to other companies. The sums due to each company were then calculated and either paid or claimed by Southern Railways.

Bletchingley on Fair Day in 1907. Note that every form of transport within sight is horse-powered. These traditional rural events survived the coming of the steam age, *but were unable to compete with the enormous growth of population that followed the advent of commuting.*

only carried the bricks out, but brought in the huge quantities of coal needed to fire the brick kilns.

Nutfield also had a brickworks built alongside the railway, as did Godstone, Ockley, Brockham and Shalford. North of the Downs, Epsom had two brickworks in the later 19th century. Both had private sidings, but neither seems to have moved many bricks out by rail. The railways brought in the coal for the firing process but the bricks were mostly used locally in the building boom that was then taking place.

A novel twist to the brickworks-railway combination was provided by the John Earley Cook works just outside Oxshott. This works had a private siding through which coal was brought in and bricks taken out. The unique aspect of the works was the fact that vast quantities of domestic rubbish from London were brought in by rail to be burned on the site. The resulting ash was then mixed in with brick clay to produce a lighter, cheaper form of brick.

There was one industry in Surrey that very definitely avoided the advantages of the age of steam — at least to start with — it was one centred on the banks of the Tillingbourne stream just east of Shalford. Established by the East India Company in the 1600s this works produced gunpowder. No iron or steel was allowed on the site, nor were fires. All the movement of heavy loads of charcoal, sulphur or saltpetre around the site was made in wooden trucks running on wooden tracks with the metal fittings and components made of brass. Perhaps understandably, the management of the gunpowder works wanted little to do with steam railways which not only had high temperature fires throwing out sparks, but relied on steel tracks and iron trucks that might create a spark at any moment.

Similar precautions were taken at the nearby Chilworth Gunpowder Mill, but on at least one occasion they were not enough. On 12 February 1901 one of the workrooms was torn apart by a massive blast that sent a column of smoke hundreds of feet into the air. Working inside the building had been three men, all of whom were killed. Bits and pieces of their bodies were found as much as 100 feet away from the demolished workroom. Pushing a wooden cart past at the time had been three other men, all likewise killed. A subsequent inquiry was held and found that all safety procedures had been in place and were being followed carefully. Perhaps it had just been bad luck.

A freight train waits just outside South Croydon in 1920. Unlike most other railways, the LB&SCR always gained most of its revenue from passenger traffic, with freight being a secondary business.

Oxted station in about 1902. Although there are passengers in evidence in this photo, the main business on the line at this date was *freight with large quantities of bricks being transported out of the area to help build the rapidly expanding London suburbs.*

In 1885 the SER built a siding to supply the works with materials and to take out the finished explosives. Even then, the materials were moved from the siding to the works in the traditional wood and brass vehicles. Not until new forms of explosive, such as cordite, began to be made did steam power enter the works itself. These new explosives were more stable than gunpowder and so accidents were less likely.

A similarly explosive business was opened adjacent to Holmwood Station in 1933. This was the Schermuly Pistol Rocket Works which produced flares, verey lights and similar devices. Gunpowders was brought in by special train in sealed, spark proof trucks. The finished products were taken out again in similarly careful conditions.

Not all industries did well out of the age of steam. One of the first to suffer was the charcoal business. This had been a lucrative trade in the forested Weald and on the wooded lowlands north of the Downs for centuries. Charcoal had been produced on a near industrial scale during Roman times and by the later medieval period was again a prosperous trade. The main market for Surrey charcoal was the local iron industry, but after that collapsed charcoal was shipped to London. There the charcoal was widely used for cooking and

The down express thunders through Woking in 1950. The coming of the steam railways heralded a host of wide ranging social changes in Surrey - none of which had been foreseen and few desired by those who built the railways.

craftwork purposes. In the better houses charcoal was used for heating, but more humble dwellings burned logs. And log-cutting was another profitable business in the Surrey woodlands.

The age of steam brought such businesses to a sudden halt. Coal brought down by ship from Newcastle had long been a rival to more local wood and charcoal, but the price difference had not been so great as to give coal the edge. The advent of steam operated railways made coal much cheaper to transport from mine to market. There was a sudden collapse in charcoal and firewood sales to London. As the railways pushed out into Surrey itself, coal became much cheaper across the county. The charcoal business came to a sudden end.

In the later decades of the 19th century, mined coal grew to be the main source of heat in all domestic properties across Surrey. The transport of coal for domestic heating and cooking ranges was to be one of the most profitable aspects of the steam railways for much of their existence. When most homes switched to electricity and gas, the demand for coal slumped and with it profits for the railways with far reaching consequences.

The Leisure Lines

Although the vast majority of railway lines in the age of steam were built for sound commercial reasons based on industry, agriculture or trade, there were a few that were built for rather more frivolous reasons. Surrey has quite a few of these lines that were built not for trade or industry, but for pleasure.

The first was the LSWR line to Hampton Court. The great Tudor palace of Hampton Court actually stands on the north bank of the Thames, in Middlesex, but there is a road bridge just west of the palace that links it to Surrey. The reason for the interest of the LSWR in Hampton Court was that in 1838 Queen Victoria had opened the grounds and state rooms to the public. The proximity to London made the palace a popular day out for urban folk. An estimated 180,000 people were coming each year, and the LSWR management wanted to get some of the business transporting them.

The company chairman, W.J. Chapman, however, was unconvinced. He did not think that a line dedicated to passengers only would make much of a profit. He was eventually convinced to give the go ahead when persuaded that the line would improve the reputation of the company by providing "a fresh means of cheap and legitimate recreation for the poorer classes."

It was decided to begin the branch line from the main line just west of what is now Surbiton. The branch line then ran along an embankment over the flat land for almost two miles until it came down to ground level on the south bank of the Thames adjacent to the road bridge. Because the line was facing a royal palace, and because it

A 1958 ticket from Egham to Ascot. The great race course at Ascot was served by the line from Waterloo through Egham.

Although the sign behind these fashionably dressed bathers reads "Palm Beach", the youngsters are actually splashing about in the River Thames at Thames Ditton. In 1926, when this picture was taken, the village was a popular destination for day trippers on sunny weekends.

was intended almost exclusively for passengers, the company decided to spend rather more than was usual on the station. The architect Sir William Tite was brought in to design the terminal. He constructed a handsome two-story building in red brick with white stone quoining and ornamental gable ends — all to blend in with the mighty palace over the river. The engine shed was given a similarly ornate facade, though the sides and rear were severely plain. There were two platforms, one shorter than the other.

The flow of sightseers going to Hampton Court boomed when the railway opened. Not only did most of those who had been going to the palace anyway choose to go by rail, but so did thousands of others who had not previously thought of visiting. By 1865 of the 95 trains leaving the LSWR London terminus at the weekend, no fewer than 26 went to Hampton Court.

In November 1851 a station was opened half way along the branch line and named Thames Ditton. The name was taken from a small village beside the Thames about half a mile from the station. The village had acquired a number of prestige houses together with a scattering of hotels and was well on the way to becoming a minor weekend resort. The station was a much more subdued affair than that at Hampton Court. The stationmaster's house and the station were plain brick buildings set into the embankment with the platforms built above them.

In the 1890s the ever increasing flow of passengers led to a rebuilding of Hampton Court station. The original building was extended — though in rather more humble style. The two platforms were replaced by three platforms and four sidings. A goods yard was added, together with a spur line that ran down to a wharf on the Thames.

The innovative ways in which the LSWR and other railway companies sought to boost their trade during this period is shown by the "tour tickets" that were sold. In the case of Hampton Court, the ticket carried the passenger from London to Hampton Court by rail, from Hampton Court to Windsor by paddle steamer and then from Windsor back to London by rail. A grand day out indeed.

The modern Epsom Downs Station as it appeared in 2009. The original station was demolished in the 1980s to make way for an extensive housing estate built over the old sidings and other areas. This building was erected to serve as the new station, but is now a nursery school.

An LB&SCR train prepares to leave Croydon West for Epsom Downs on 1906. This is one of the regular services, not a race day special, so it consists of only one carriage hauled by a 'Terrier' tank engine. Station staff stand beside the train and the engine driver peers from his cab.

The daytripper trade to Hampton Court received a huge boost when the Hurst Park racecourse was opened in 1889. The course lay on the south bank of the Thames about a mile west of the station. It covered 120 acres and was built complete with grandstand and paddock. The prosperity of the racecourse peaked in the Edwardian period. The LSWR considered extending the branch line to the racecourse, but so many people had by this date built houses or shops around the Hampton Court station to cater to the daytrippers that the cost of buying up the properties and demolishing them to make way for the extension was prohibitive. Instead two more sidings were installed at Hampton Court on which race day specials could await their return passengers. In 1914 a total of 50 special trains were run on the Whitsun holiday when a major race meeting coincided with an event at the palace. A special signal box was erected at Thames Ditton, though it was manned only on race days.

In 1875 a racecourse was opened adjacent to Ditton Marsh station, soon to be renamed Esher. The Sandown Park venture was an entirely new concept in horse racing, and one that proved to be hugely popular. The land in question was at the time owned by the Church of England — and had been ever since it had formed part of a minor priory in the middle ages. The developer took out a long lease and began the conversion of the park into a race course.

The innovative aspect of Sandown Park was that the entire grounds of the racecourse were enclosed within high fences and the public charged an admission fee — such a thing had never happened before. The move made the racecourse both safer and more respectable than the other courses of the time. Sandown began to attract middle class race-goers and families on a day out. This success persuaded the Church of England to sell the site — those in charge felt it inappropriate that the Church should make a profit from gambling, even indirectly.

In 1882 the LSWR built two additional platforms at Esher for race days only, together with two large sidings on which race trains could be parked while awaiting returning passengers. As at Thames Ditton an additional signal box was put in to be used on race days only. The situation at Esher was complicated by the fact that this was a main line station and that express through trains could not be disrupted by the large number of stopping race trains. The following year a tunnel was bored through the embankment to provide a direct pedestrian link into the racecourse from the race platforms, cutting out the need for racegoers to walk a half mile by road to reach the elaborate wrought iron main gates into Sandown Park on the Portsmouth Road.

Landowner and MP, Cosmo Bonsor was the main mover behind the building of the railway up the Chipstead Valley to emerge on to the Epsom Downs at Tattenham Corner.

Derby Day 1909 looking towards Tattenham Corner. The horses are approaching the finish line in the centre of the picture. The main stands are to the left of the picture while the crowds on the right are filling the open common land where access was free.

In 1888 the entire station superstructure was rebuilt. This was partly to cater for the race day traffic, partly to fit the buildings better to the new platform layout and partly to enable the LSWR to install prestige royal waiting rooms for the benefit of the Duchess of Albany, who lived at nearby Claremont House, and her numerous high society visitors. The resulting buildings were spacious and comfortable, but remarkably dull to look at.

It was these buildings that were at Esher when I first began using the trains to commute up to London. The old royal waiting room was still there, though it had been stripped of its more upmarket fittings by my day. There was a large fireplace set in the wall, but it was never lit even on the coldest of days. Still, at least the waiting room meant that I was able to get out of the biting wind that howled around in winter time. I also remember the rather odd positioning of the ticket office. It took the form of a squared brick structure set into the embankment under the down platform. On one side a door opened on to the staircase that led up to the platform. On a second side a door gave access to the lane that ran through a brick-arched tunnel through the embankment. A third door opened out on to a fairly extensive cobbled forecourt. In my day the forecourt was used as a taxi rank and car park, but it had originally been constructed so that the Duchess of Albany had somewhere for her carriage to turn around and wait.

Those old buildings were all swept away in 1987 — by which time I was commuting from Surbiton — and replaced by a modern red-brick and glass structure designed for the motor car, not the horse carriage. The old sidings were replaced by an extensive car park, which was quickly full every day. The old waiting room was demolished along with the huge canopies over the platforms. Both were replaced by bus-shelter style structures that could hold only a fraction of the commuters who used the platforms on busy days — and even then a gap at ground level allowed the wind to whip around the ankles.

The successes of Hurst Park and Sandown Park prompted the construction of another racecourse adjacent to a railway at Lingfield, on the LB&SCR line to East Grinstead. As at Hurst Park, a branch line to the race course was considered, but the distance was only 600 yards so the LB&SCR never went ahead with the plan. The LB&SCR did, however, make changes to the existing Lingfield station. The platforms were lengthened and a loop and siding

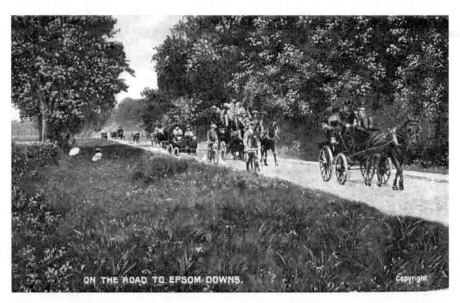

ON THE ROAD TO EPSOM DOWNS.

A procession of eager race-goers advance along the road from Epsom railway station to the racecourse on the downs south of the town in 1902. The most famous race held here was, and remains, the Derby when tens of thousands flocked out of London to the Epsom Downs.

Tadworth Station in 2010. The building no longer serves as a station and for some years was rented out as commercial property, but by 2009 was empty and boarded up. The platforms are now accessed via a separate entrance and are served by ticket machines.

installed. What had been a freight loading dock was converted to make it suitable for the loading and unloading of horses, tackle and other race gear. Finally a covered walkway was installed to the course, but this was for the use of members of the race club only. Members of the public had to walk along Station Road exposed to the elements.

Because of its location, Lingfield attracted race day specials from Brighton as well as from London. This rather complicated the logistics of organising the race trains as they arrived and left from two different directions. The LB&SCR decided to move all the specials awaiting return passengers down the line to East Grinstead rather than go to the trouble of building additional sidings at Lingfield.

The great race courses of Ascot and Kempton Park are not in Surrey, but the rail lines that serve them do run through the county. The race day specials that served the two courses were a major boost to the lines in Surrey, with Ascot attracting 40 specials on Gold Cup Day in the 1890s.

By far the largest and most popular race course in Surrey, however, has always been Epsom Downs. Unlike the park racecourses at Sandown, Kempton and Lingfield, the course at Epsom was laid out across the open Downs. Only the grandstand, paddock and adjacent areas were fenced in and an entrance fee charged. The rest is publicly accessible land across which anyone could, and can still, wander to watch the racing.

I now live only about 300 yards from Epsom racecourse and although I am not a keen race-goer I frequently pop up to see the races. On occasional days in the summer there are race meetings on weekday afternoons that stretch on into the early evening. I collect my daughter from her school and then we walk up the hill to the racecourse to watch a few races, buy an ice cream from the van parked in a layby and have a bit of time together.

Racing had been established here centuries before the age of steam arrived, and the railways sought to take advantage of it. In 1838 the London and Southampton Railway (later the LSWR) advertised a special Derby Day Ticket that would take passengers from London to Surbiton by rail, and from there to Epsom Downs by horse-drawn road coach. Far more people turned up than could be carried on the trains and the police had to be called to pacify the

Coldharbour in 1933. This village at the foot of Leith Hill enjoyed a boom in weekend business as a result of hikers *stopping here for refreshments in the course of their rambles around the county.*

Virginia Water station in around 1912 with an "Up" train from Chertsey stopped at the platform on its way to London. The stationmaster stands by the cafe while two porters are on the platform offering to help passengers.

resulting protests.

When the LB&SCR Epsom station opened in 1847 in Epsom town centre, this meant that there was only a walk of less than two miles from rail to racecourse. As with the 1838 train and coach special, the crowds overwhelmed the station staff. Dozens, perhaps hundreds of "roughs" got on to the trains without paying by clambering over the station fences. The following year the LB&SCR were ready. They smeared the tops of the fences with tar, in which were set sharp hooks. Suspecting that this might not be enough they scoured the network for big, burly porters and took them all down to Epsom for Derby Day. At Epsom the men were issued with cudgels and told to keep order, keep out anyone who had not paid for a ticket and not to be too squeamish about it. The policy worked. Order was kept and fares collected. One hesitates to think what health and safety officials would make of such a scheme today.

These race day specials were not enough, however, and in 1861 the LB&SCR decided to build a special line for the racecourse. The 4 mile dual line left the mainline at Sutton, heading south on a steep gradient to negotiate a succession of cuttings, embankments and towering bridges to clamber up on to the summit of the Downs and end just 200 yards from the racecourse.

Predictably business was slack on most days of the year, with only 30 passengers buying tickets for the average day. On race days, however, things were very different. For the race meeting of May 1865 which lasted just 6 days no less than 70,000 people passed through Epsom Downs station. On top of that there were hundreds of horses and truckloads of tackle, fodder and other necessary gear. To cope with all this movement, the station had nine platforms, five sidings, a coal stage, a tank house and a turntable. There were also three signal boxes, manned only on race days, to handle the huge number of trains and the movements that they involved.

Published on 23 July 1947, this special timetable for Southern trains running over the August bank holiday contains 76 pages of timetables, instructions to drivers as to where to leave their locomotives at close of day and other technical instructions. Although many special trains were run over this bank holiday, the glory days of specials were over as fewer and fewer people took the train out of London on daytrips.

What did not exist was a proper station building as the rail company had not thought it cost-effective to build one for the few days it would be used. Instead there was a small building where tickets could be purchased and some awning that was put up on race days. Temporary marquees were put up on the Downs adjacent to the station where travellers could buy food and drink. Thousands of pints of beer were sold and vast quantities of sandwiches and other snacks served to the race goers as they passed through.

In 1890 the Prince of Wales, the future King Edward VII, began using Epsom Downs Station arriving on the Royal Train. That encouraged the LB&SCR to start laying on First Class only race day specials composed exclusively of Pullman coaches. Less exalted passengers arrived in more modest carriages.

The former home of George Meredith was an important attraction for daytrippers coming to the Boxhill and West Humble station in the early 20th century. The great novelist died in 1909 and his house was almost at once opened to the public.

Even with all these special trains to Epsom Downs, thousands of race goers still travelled to Epsom town station and walked up the hill. The fact that the town had numerous pubs and eateries no doubt encouraged many to follow this route, but it was undeniable that the Epsom Downs station simply could not cope. The fact came to the attention of the delightfully named local MP Cosmo Bonsor, who was also a Director of the Bank of England. Bonsor had for some time been trying to interest somebody in building a railway up the Chipstead Valley which would be conveniently sited close to his home and be of benefit to his tenants and other local farmers and businesses.

The promise of huge race day crowds added to the passenger and freight traffic generated by the valley residents was what Bonsor needed to make a financially viable case for the proposed railway. Construction costs were estimated at £250,000, the SER agreed to pay for the alterations necessary at Purley for the new line to junction with their existing tracks. The prospectus was a success and investors money came in. In November 1897 the Chipstead Valley Railway (CVR) was opened as far as Kingswood. In 1899 the SER gained a new board member: Cosmo Bonsor MP.

The CVR line was pushed forward to Tadworth in 1900 and the following year was completed to the racecourse itself, with the terminal station being built a stone's throw from Tattenham Corner, after which it was named. It was on these final sections of the track that the main engineering works were needed, as the line clawed its way up on to the high Downs. There were numerous cuttings, the Tadworth Station was built entirely inside one, and several embankments. There were also two tunnels. The longer one was named "Kingswood", while the shorter one was dubbed "Hoppity".

The terminal at Tattenham Corner was built to be more attractive to race goers than the rival at LB&SCR's Epsom Downs. If the proximity to the race course were not enough, the station had platforms 20 feet wide and 750 feet long. There were six passenger platforms, plus a seventh for horses and other race trade. Beside the horse platform were stables for the horses, bedrooms for jockeys and stableboys, plus offices for the horse owners — who were presumably expected to stay in more salubrious hotels nearby. There were also seven sidings where trains could wait for returning passengers, plus a turntable. On Derby Day itself this was not enough and special trains were parked on the down line in readiness for the mass exodus in the evening.

Between the platforms were additional release lines along which locomotives could move to get from one end of their train of coaches to the other.

Unlike at Epsom Downs, Tattenham Corner had a proper station building — albeit one of wooden construction with a slate roof. There was a ticket office, concourse, refreshment room, staff restaurant and possibly the largest male toilets on any station on

The large cutting just outside Tadworth Station was necessary to enable the tracks to claw their way up from Kingswood, through Tadworth and on to the Epsom Downs. The gradient here is the steepest along the Tattenham branch line.

The entrance to the delightfully named Hoppity Tunnel on the branch line to Tattenham Corner was the major engineering work on this line, constructed largely to transport crowds to the racecourse up on Epsom Downs.

the network — no doubt a necessary addition give the amounts of beer traditionally consumed at the races. In previous decades the scattered patches of shrubs and copses of trees had been good enough, but by the end of the 19th century the increasingly numbers of middle class gents arriving for the racing demanded something better.

The large area covered by the platforms, sidings and station had to be level, but the land was not. The large amounts of chalk that had to be excavated away was formed into a large, grass covered mound in front of the station that offered magnificent views across the race course to the finishing line. It was reserved for senior management of the railway company and their guests. Today such exalted guests flock to the sumptuous corporate hospitality suites at the two grandstands near the finishing line. The grassy bund is open to the public and is always packed on race days.

The busiest year for Tattenham Corner station was 1925. On Derby Day no less than 115 race day specials came to the station, carrying a total of over 50,000 race goers. The less busy Epsom Downs station still managed to cater for 54 trains carrying 20,000 people. At least as many again travelled to Epsom and walked up the hill to the race course. These trains were, on average, only 2 minutes late. Given the hugely complex task of organising all these train movements that was an amazing achievement that the railways today would do well to match.

It was not only palaces and sport that brought day trippers to Surrey stations. Many people from London delighted in taking a train out to Guildford, Reigate or Dorking for the day, but most preferred to head for the scenic beauty of the North Downs. The peaks of Box Hill and Leith Hill proved to be the most popular targets for London day trippers. Leith Hill was served by Holmwood station, about two miles away. Boxhill, however, had its own station.

The first "Box Hill" station was, in fact, at Dorking and is now known as Dorking Deepdene. It was opened in February 1851 as "Box Hill and Leatherhead Road" on the SER line from Reading to Redhill. This distinguished it from the Dorking Town (now Dorking West) station that had opened in July 1849. The name was no doubt chosen with an eye to the tourist trade. Box Hill was already a famous beauty spot and had featured in one of Jane Austen's books as a favoured picnicking spot for the Surrey gentry.

Visitors arriving at "Box Hill and Leatherhead Road" found themselves faced by a walk of over a mile down the Mole Valley before they reached the foot of the hill. The walk did not put off the younger daytrippers. On a Sunday evening in August 1851 three draper's assistants from London were arrested at the station. They had arrived at the station as a train was preparing to leave and proceeded to "obstruct the stationmaster in the execution of his duty", whatever that meant. Presumably they had been drinking. They were fined five shillings each by way of punishment.

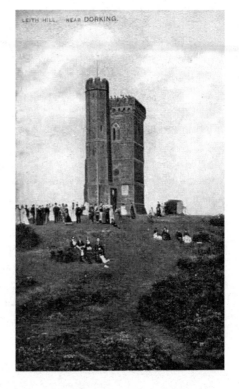

The tower that marks the summit of Leith Hill in 1902. The daytrippers who came out from London made climbing up this towering hill to enjoy the views a central feature of a day out. The majority of these energetic pleasure seekers came to Holmwood station, about two miles from the hill.

The stand maintained by the Ramblers Association on Box Hill Station at weekends and bank holidays. The volunteers of the association handing out maps and advice leaflets are (from left to right) Bernard, Winnie and Ron Foyle with Miss Chipchord behind the table.

In 1867 the more convenient "West Humble for Box Hill" station (now Box Hill and West Humble) opened almost at the foot of the hill. The new station was an instant success with the daytrippers. Visitors of all ages began arriving in ever increasing numbers. By 1890 the average bank holiday saw 5,000 people buy tickets from London stations to West Humble for Box Hill. Extra trains began to be laid on to cope with the crowds.

On the August bank holiday of 1891 came a Box Hill outing that few would ever forget. The trades union the United Society of Boiler Makers and Iron Shipbuilders decided to organise a day out for their members working in London's docklands. The scheme was a huge success and over 5,000 tickets were sold. The union turned to the LB&SCR who laid on a number of special trains to run from London Bridge to West Humble and Box Hill. On the appointed day the day trippers formed up in the early morning outside the gates of the East India Dock. Led by a marching band and with their union banners waving cheerfully in the breeze the crowd set off to march to the station and board their trains.

Unfortunately nobody had thought to tell the good folk of West Humble or Dorking what was coming. When the specials arrived, the 5,000 men, women and children from the East End poured out to join the already sizeable bank holiday crowds. Large as Box Hill was and experienced as the locals were at catering to daytrippers, neither could cope. The open slopes of the hills were thick with people, the pubs ran dry of drink and empty of bread. Thousands surged into Dorking to find food and drink, flooding the town's streets with a tide of humanity.

By evening the happy Eastenders were linking arms to march up and down the streets. Others were holding impromptu singing concerts, belting out music hall favourites with a fine disregard for tuneful singing. Elsewhere the youngsters were dancing on the pavements and along the streets. Nobody seems to have been deliberately destructive, but with all the high jinks and heavy drinking going on there were inevitable accidents. Men toppled off walls into gardens, dancers bumped into pedestrians and promenaders lost their way. There were no arrests, but there were numerous complaints about petty damage and misbehaviour. Finally the special trains pulled in to take the revellers home. Most of them swayed back on board, only a few were too sozzled to make it and spent the night sleeping on benches.

The numbers of visitors continued to increase, and with them the pubs and tea rooms established to cater for them. In 1938 the August bank holiday saw

Punch Bowl Hindhead.

The Devil's Punchbowl near Hindhead was a major attraction during the heyday of hiking and cycling in Surrey during the 1920s. Thousands of Londoners boarded trains to the Surrey countryside to enjoy a day out among the rolling hills.

a peak of over 10,000 Londoners arrive at Dorking or West Humble to enjoy a day out. By that date the hobby of hiking had become popular. Maps and leaflets showing scenic walks in the Surrey hills were available at London stations to encourage those seeking a healthy day out to go to stations other than those serving the famous Box Hill. Organised tours were laid on by enterprising locals who advertised guided hikes with the main points of interest being pointed out to Londoners down for the day and lunch being served at a convenient pub. A typical 10 shilling day out would include rail tickets to Gomshall, a four mile walk to a pub for lunch, followed by three miles to a tea room for tea and cake, followed by another four mile stretch back to Gomshall for the train back to London.

Special trains were laid on for summer weekends to carry hikers out to the Surrey Downs. As the trains rattled south, railway staff would go along the corridors handing out leaflets and maps about the guided walks, sites to be visited and hostelries to be enjoyed. The take up among those wanting to follow their own walking routes was boosted by the provision of "go as you please" returns which were valid for the outward journey to a named station

Locomotive 32342 stops at Tattenham Corner in 1948. Although the line to this station had been electrified in the 1920s, a lack of modern electric trains meant that steam engines were prominent on the line in the postwar period.

The locomotive 7813 Freshford Manor pulls a down passenger express train into Reigate on 2 July 1963. By this date only a very few passenger trains on Surrey railways were *hauled by steam locomotives as the switchover to electric units was nearing completion.*

and a return that evening from any station in Surrey. Those tickets soon became favourites with cyclists who could cover long distances along country lanes during the day.

At the peak of the hiking craze in the 1930s some 30,000 tickets were sold to walkers and cyclists each dry weekend in the summer.

The railway companies were also looking to maximise the income from the race course tracks that were busy only on race days. The LB&SCR laid on "Children's Treat" days at Epsom Downs station. These consisted of day trips from central London to the rural station where the travellers would find slides, swings, roundabouts, pony rides, organised ball games and a host of other child-related attractions. Refreshments were strictly alcohol-free with tea tents and sweet counters available and no local pubs open for business.

The Treats excursions were often organised by Sunday Schools based in the East End of London to give their pupils an exciting and healthy day out in the country. The LB&SCR advertised through the Church of England and nonconformist chapels offering special cheap tickets for organised groups booking in advance to travel on Children's Treat special trains. In 1885 the average Sunday saw 1,000 children and around 200 adults arriving to enjoy the wholesome day out. Similar Treats days were soon being organised by other companies for less busy stations in rural locations.

Among the longest serving steam locomotives to run on Surrey rails were the freight engines of the H15 class built for the LSWR before the First World War. A total of 25 of these 4-6-0 locomotives were constructed. They were notable for the fact that some of the controls were placed so high up that only drivers over 6 feet tall could reach them - other drivers were provided with a wooden stool on which to stand. This engine was photographed in 1914 as it left the factory.

A day trip of an altogether more sombre kind was promoted by the LSWR, leading to the construction of not just a new station at Brookwood, west of Woking, but also a branch line with two specialist stations. The unusual journeys were the business of the London Necropolis Company (LNC), established in 1852 to answer a pressing need in London.

For centuries the people of London had been buried in the churchyards of their parishes with no real problems, other than during the Great Plague of 1665. However, by the mid 19th century two factors were causing problems. The first was the growing population, which meant an increased number of corpses. The second was the growing fashion for installing gravestones on graves. Previously bodies were buried in unmarked plots, with memorial tablets put in the church for those who could afford them. Only the very richest had tombs or family crypts, usually inside the church itself. The growing use of gravestones by even quite humble folk meant that the churchyards were filling up with graves that could not be reused even long after the body within had mouldered away.

The aim of the LNC was to provide a vast, well organised graveyard in a rural location where London's dead could be buried beneath fitting monuments. They therefore bought 2,200 acres of Surrey countryside near the village of Brookwood, conveniently close to the LSWR main line from

London to Salisbury. In the event only 450 acres would be used for a cemetery, the rest being sold off for other purposes. A branch line was built off the main line heading southeast from Brookwood to enter the huge cemetery. There were two stations. The North Station was for the convenience of Catholics and non-conformists, while South Station was for Anglicans.

The LNC built a private station in London, alongside Waterloo in York Street. This allowed the grieving relatives to board the train in privacy. Each train was composed of one hearse van for the carriage of up to 24 coffins and a number of passenger coaches for the mourners. All the carriages on these trains were painted and decorated in suitably funereal colours and motifs. Additional trains were laid on for relatives to visit the graves of those already buried. The first funeral train ran in November 1854.

In 1864 the LSWR built Brookwood station where the funeral branch line left the mainline. The station was originally intended for the convenience of mourners or those visiting graves who were coming from places other than London who wanted to transfer to trains out of London working the branch line. It soon began to function as a station serving the local area. In 1902 the LSWR wanted to enlarge Waterloo Station, so the company bought the LNC station and built the funeral company a new station and office complex nearby complete with an imposing entrance archway. Business was brisk, and remained so even after cremation became legal and the overcrowding of London parish churchyards ceased to be such a problem.

Chapter 5

The Coming of the Commuters

For most of the millennia that mankind has been on Earth the vast majority of people have lived within a few yards of where they worked. The earliest farmers lived on their farms, as farmers do today. When the need arose for specialist craftsmen such as blacksmiths, wheelwrights or potters to service the agricultural communities, they set up workshops in their homes. Even when the first factories employing hundreds of people were established in the 18th century, the workers still chose to live just down the road. Most factories were quickly surrounded by tenements and terraced housing. Even the factory owners lived nearby so that they could trot in on their horses to supervise the workers.

The age of steam changed it all forever — and Surrey was to change more than most.

The cities where the factories were based had become progressively bigger, dirtier and smellier than they had ever been before. And no city was bigger, smellier and dirtier than London. Living in London was not an enjoyable experience. For gentry and factory owners the problem could be got around without too much trouble. They could afford fast horses and comfortable carriages that made it feasible to travel up to a dozen miles to work daily. Others chose to live deeper in the countryside, travelling to work on a Monday and staying in rooms for the week before returning home for weekends.

For most workers, however, this was impossible. Keeping a horse — and still more a carriage — was a massively expensive thing to do. Nearly everybody had to walk, which meant living close to the place of work.

The railways made it possible, for the first time ever, for reasonably humble workers to live in one place and then travel to work in another. This habit of commuting, as it became known, was fairly slow to get started. Railway companies had not planned to cater for commuters, because none existed when the railways were built. The railways were designed for freight and for travellers. The idea of a mass of people wanting to travel one way at 8am and then back the other at 6pm had never been considered and did not feature in the timetables.

It was around 1880 or so that commuting began to feature as a distinct activity in Surrey. The impulse came not from the railways themselves, but from house builders. It was these developers who spotted the social trend of commuting and set out to cash in. At first it was considered that the best way to make money was to build detached villas suitable for upper tiers of management or senior clerks. These were the type of family men who would keep a couple of full time servants, plus two or more part time domestic help. They were not business owners, but they did seek to emulate their social and financial betters. Such men, often urged on by the wives it would seem, were keen to move out of London but were tied to a daily appearance in the office. Commuting was the answer.

At first it was the railway lines that had been built for other purposes, and the stations on them, that saw the boom in commuter traffic. The station at Ashtead, for instance, was opened in 1859 on the original Epsom to Leatherhead line. It remained a quiet and little used rural stop until 1881 when the house developers moved in. The roads between the station and the village, over half a mile to the south, were quickly lined by substantial detached houses, each set in a good sized garden. Each house was of a distinct design. They were quickly snapped up by senior London-based workers.

James Forbes, Chairman of the Metropolitan District Railway, who was instrumental in persuading the LSWR to build a railway line to Guildford by way of Claygate and Clandon.

The influx of prosperous middle class Londoners led to a business boom in the village itself.

The high street, known here simply as The Street, saw its houses all converted to shops, with several older houses torn down to be replaced by purpose built stores. Butchers, bakers, grocers and others all enjoyed a prosperous time. There was also an increased need for gardeners, maids and casual staff of all kinds. The shop workers and domestic staff all had to live somewhere, so a string of smaller houses were built packed into narrow streets off the village centre.

The population boom in Ashtead was impressive. In 1881 the census records 926 people resident in the parish. By the time of the census of 1921 the population had increased to 3,226. Not all these people commuted, only a minority of them did, but it was the commuters who built the community and who provided the financial spring that made it all possible.

The financial profits made by both rail companies and landowners from such early commuter developments were noticed by many. Among those who took note were a trio of Surrey-based members of the House of Lords: William King-Noel, Earl of Lovelace, William Onslow, Earl of Onslow, and Henry Foley, the Baron Foley. What united these three very different men was that they each owned large tracts of land in Surrey that stretched across the picturesque hills that lie between the valleys of the Wey and Mole. The land was reasonably profitable as farming and forestry land, but not excessively so. The boom in property prices at Ashtead and elsewhere convinced Lovelace, Onslow and Foley that their lands would be worth a fortune if only they could get a railway built across them.

A Southern Railways Third Class ticket to Oxted. By the 1930s the designation of Third Class had become something of an anachronism as few, if any, trains had Second Class carriages any longer.

One of the last Third Class carriages to run on Surrey railways was this Third brake s40705 photographed at Guildford in 1961.

Unfortunately for the three lords, none of them knew anything at all about railways. But Lovelace did know James Forbes, Chairman of the Metropolitan District Railway (MDR). The MDR had been founded in 1864 to build an underground line in central London. The railway built what is now the section of the District Line from Putney Bridge to Tower Hill with a branch to Kensington and another to Hammersmith. When Lovelace contacted Forbes, the MDR was planning to extend south of the Thames to Wimbledon and to Richmond. Would the MDR want to expand even further, Lovelace wanted to know.

The answer was a rather disappointing "no", but all was not lost. The MDR was interested in building a line to Kingston and was willing to operate a line from Kingston to Guildford, if Lovelace, Foley and Onslow could raise the money to build it. Forbes advised the three noblemen that they needed to get the support of other landowners and the town councils involved if they were to stand any chance of success. The town councils of Kingston and Guildford proved to be enthusiastic. Although their towns were already served by the LSWR they considered that a second line would provide both more trains and competitive pricing. The mayors of the two towns joined the three noblemen on a committee set up to promote the provisionally named Guildford, Kingston and London Railway (GKLR).

The committee called in a surveyor who tentatively suggested a route for MDR lines from Putney to Kingston, then a route for the GKLR to run southwest through Claygate, Oxshott, Cobbham, Horsley and Clandon to Guildford. In an effort to get support from Leatherhead, a branch line to that town from Horsley was suggested. A second branch to Ashtead was also surveyed while a spur was intended to link to the LB&SCR line to Horsham. This new line was planned to run right through the heart of the LSWR territory, and Forbes advised his noble collaborators that some sort of response from the LSWR could be expected.

The board of the LSWR had indeed been following the development of the GKLR proposals with interest. They did in fact have an already approved plan for a line from Leatherhead to Guildford that was to have followed a route very similar to the southern section of the GKLR. The line had been shelved in 1859 as the projected profits from freight and passengers to be expected from the rural area had not justified the expense of construction. Now,

Situated just north of Woldingham Station the Woldingham Viaduct consists of four massive brick arches that carry the railway over the valley that runs from Woldingham to Caterham.

Seen from above the entrance to the Woldingham Tunnel, the great cutting through the Surrey hills curves away northward towards Woldingham Station.

Caterham Station staff in 1894. In its early years the Caterham line had struggled to make a profit, but by the time this photo was taken Caterham was a booming and increasingly busy commuter station. The stationmaster, Mr Foweraker, is the man in the top hat while his staff wear peaked caps.

The gentleman on the left in a flat-crowned bowker hat appears to be an official from the SER. Note that among the 14 station staff are three "boys", who would today be considered far too young to be in full time employment.

however, the situation was different. Profits to be made from commuter traffic made the line more viable, while the desire to stop a rival company getting a hold on LSWR territory made it desirable. Talks opened between the LSWR and the committee sponsoring the GKLR. The upshot of the talks was an agreement under which the GKLR would sell out to the LSWR on condition that the larger company built a line to run from Surbiton to Guildford along, more or less, the route backed by the GKLR.

There would be a branch to Leatherhead via Bookham, but the other spurs and branches were abandoned. As part of the arrangement, two private sidings were to be constructed. The first was at Clandon and was to be reserved for the exclusive use of the Earl of Onslow, whose palatial home of Clandon House lay less than a mile to the south. The second was at Horsley for the use of the Earl of Lovelace to serve his home at Horsley Towers.

The public stations along the line were to be at Claygate, Cobham, Horsley, Clandon and London Road (just outside Guildford). Effingham Junction was built where the branch from Leatherhead joined the main line and a station was erected at Bookham between Leatherhead and Effingham Junction. All three lords made huge amounts of money selling their land to property developers.

It was not only the local lords who earned money. At Cobham the arrival of the railway in 1885 saw over 200 acres up for auction as prime land for house building. The development of the villages of Cobham — they were in fact three small hamlets named Cobham Tilt, Cobham Street and Cobham — went ahead steadily with most of the houses being built to a similarly spacious design as at Ashtead. The development of the land around Oxshott Station, the stop about 2 miles closer to London than Cobham, was at first hampered by the fact that the majority of the land was in the hands of the Crown. The Crown Estates were reluctant to let the land on long leases and refused to sell it, while developers saw no profit in building on short lease land. It was not until the 1920s that the impasse was solved. Thereafter development of large, luxurious houses set in large gardens on private estates got underway.

At Claygate, closer still to London, development began on Lord Foley's land as soon as the railway arrived. The Foley Arms Hotel was erected to cater to those arriving by train and to the new local residents — and service it still provides. A little nest of six new roads was laid out on farmland beside the station. The houses built here were smaller than at Ashtead, Cobham and Oxshott, though they

The 4th Earl of Onslow wearing the regalia of a senior member of the Freemasons. Onslow owned vast estates east of Guildford and made huge sums of money by selling off stretches of farmland for the construction of commuter housing.

71

were still detached. The shorter distance to London meant that tickets for commuters were cheaper, and so commuting from Claygate was an activity that was open to those lower down the pay scale. The houses were snapped up, so other developers moved in to build semi-detached houses set in less spacious plots. By 1914 there were 500 new houses in Claygate where the population had grown from 750 in 1881 to 2,800.

Other places were, at least at first, less influenced by the commuting boom. Leatherhead and Dorking were already reasonably prosperous towns, and while both towns saw a rash of house building in the final two decades of the 19th century, it would seem that most of this was to meet local demand. The increasing pace of business was, of course, largely due to the railways but the people living in the new houses tended to work locally.

From 1885 onward Guildford developers building on land formerly owned by the Earl of Onslow, specialised in large detached houses built for men who bought First Class season tickets to London. Most of these senior managers took trains that got them into London around 10am, reflecting a rather more relaxed attitude to office hours than could be afforded by those lower down the

Walton on Thames station in the later 1940s. The white paint slapped over telegraph poles and the platform edge was introduced during the war for the benefit of passengers travelling during the blackout. Many people were injured by falling off platform edges or blundering into poles.

A label to be attached to an item of luggage heading for Esher in the 1920s. The once rural village was by this date becoming the site of several exclusive housing estates and the name was becoming synonymous with genteel living.

pay scale who lived at Claygate, or even Oxshott and Cobham. Further out still at Godalming, Farnham and Haslemere the pace of development was even slower, though the houses were, if anything, even more luxurious.

Meanwhile, in eastern Surrey, the loss-making Caterham branch line was starting to turn a modest profit as commuter housing sprang up around Caterham station. The tickets bought by the commuters augmented the meagre freight takings to give the line an operating profit. The main attraction for new residents was the charming and picturesque nature of the steep, narrow valley in which Caterham stood. That valley continued some miles further south to Godstone, while similarly scenic and attractive country lay to the east and south of Caterham around Woldingham and Oxted. The SER decided that it could lucratively extend its line into the area to open up the hills for commuter housing. Unfortunately for the SER, the LB&SCR had got there first.

In 1869 the LB&SCR had bought out the ailing Surrey & Sussex Railway (SSR) which had been building a line from Croydon to Tunbridge Wells by way of Oxted when it had run into financial problems. The works had got as far as Oxted when the LB&SCR took over. The embankments, cuttings and other works had been built by navvies brought in from continental Europe, who were still on site and wanting their wages. The LB&SCR hurriedly paid off the foreigners so that they could bring in their own workforce, only to abandon the work entirely when they realised that the SSR had been hopelessly over-optimistic about the traffic the line might expect. The line had been left incomplete, but still in LB&SCR hands. Now that the SER was considering a commuter line in the area, the LB&SCR dusted off the old SSR plans.

In a highly unusual example of common sense, the SER and LB&SCR negotiated a joint deal under which commuter lines in the area would be jointly owned and operated through the Croydon, Oxted and East Grinstead Railways. The old SSR line was completed, while the Caterham branch was extended south past Godstone to connect to the SER mainline running east from Redhill.

Stations were opened at Upper Warlingham, Woldingham, Oxted, Hurst Green, Lingfield and Dormans. Of these only Dormans failed to attract new commuter housing developments. Running as they did through steep valleys and hills, the lines involved the construction of much heavy engineering work in the form of viaducts, bridges, cuttings and tunnels. These are among the most impressive railway structures in Surrey. The longest tunnel was the Woldingham Tunnel which ran through the chalk North Downs for one mile and 506 yards. The builders found that the course was riddled by underground springs and streams, which they channelled so that the water flows out of the southern end of the tunnel to fall into the headwaters of the River Eden. The tunnel collapsed in 1917 and again in 1919, after which it was rebuilt. Erosion caused by the running waters was blamed for the collapses.

The LSWR main line running from Surbiton across Surrey to Farnborough had a rather different history of commuter growth, largely due to the faster and more frequent train services offered by the company. At Esher, the former Ditton Marsh, development was slow due to the fact that the land around the station was prime farming land and the owners had no wish to sell off such a profitable business. The next stop west, Walton on Thames, had been built in open country some distance south of the village, but by 1880 was already surrounded by a scattering of houses. Over the next thirty years house building

Whyteleafe Station photographed before the First World War. A member of uniformed staff, perhaps the stationmaster, waits on the Up platform for a train to arrive.

continued quickly and by 1914 the old village was linked to the station by a continuous sprawl of housing.

The next station was Weybridge, a stop that for decades was dominated by the huge housing estate of St George's Hill that lies just to its south. This estate was laid out in 1911 by builder Walter Tarrant who was determined to construct a luxurious estate for the seriously wealthy. The estate was built around a quality, 18 hole golf course and the landscaped 520 foot tall hill that gave the estate its name. Each plot was at least an acre in size and each house was individually designed by an architect. These rules are still enforced and the residents remain wealthy.

By way of contrast, the station at Woking stood amid land owned by a company determined to make as much money as quickly as possible. It began by building the shops and commercial properties at the back of the station on cheaper land squeezed between the railway and the semi-derelict Basingstoke Canal. This odd arrangement can still be seen as the main entrance to the station from the town centre is by way of an unimposing doorway, while the major entrance faces on to a car park. Although the station was built in 1838 it was not until the 1880s that a ticket office was added on the town side. By the time the station was rebuilt in the 1930s land had become so expensive that all reconstruction had to take place on the original cramped site.

Meanwhile the development of Woking had been going on apace. When the railway first arrived there were no buildings other than the station within sight. On Hook Heath the developers tried to emulate the privileged success of St George's Hill. A golf course was laid out and plots of at least one acre in size were marked out. The estate was always rather smaller and less grand than its rival, but undoubtedly attracted to Woking the type of commuter who travelled First Class. Elsewhere, the developers were putting up smaller and cheaper houses to appeal to less wealthy commuters and to local tradesmen.

By 1911 Woking was the largest town in Surrey with a population of 28,000 —not bad for a place that had begun as a station in the middle of a desolate heath.

The carriages in which these commuters travelled were, at first, rather a mixed and haphazard collection of rolling stock. The very first passenger carriages were simply freight carts with wooden benches installed. These were used for transporting the navvies and other construction workers while the railways were being built, but a few survived to serve as cheap transport for manual workers. The upmarket carriages for travelling gentry were produced by bolting the bodies of horse-drawn carriages on to the chassis of a freight car, usually three carriage bodies per chassis. These vehicles were entirely unsprung — comfort depended entirely on the padding in the seats.

It was in the 1850s that the distinction between different classes of passenger comfort, and ticket price, was properly established. It would last for over a century until the then British Rail decided to overhaul the system again and so produce what we have today.

Most rail companies standardised passenger comfort into three categories: First Class, Second Class and Third Class. As a rule of thumb, First Class was for the gentry and Second Class was for everyone else. The Third Class carriages were for the use of workmen in dirty clothes — such as farm workers with cow muck on their boots or factory workers in overalls coated with grease. Once these men had got home, washed and changed they would travel Second Class.

On the LB&SCR, which effectively set the standard in Surrey, the chief engineer John Craven designed a range of carriages in three classes in 1851, and these continued to be made with little variation into the 1880s and were in service to the 1890s.

The Second Class carriage was that used by most commuters. It was a standard 18 feet 6 inches long and mounted on a standard, four wheeled "Craven" chassis. The carriage had a wooden body which formed one cabin, divided internally into four compartments by bench seating that ran right across the carriage. A door on either side gave access to each of the compartments. There was a single oil lamp in the centre of the carriage which was lit by the conductor at dusk and provided a fitful light to the whole carriage.

The comfort factor was limited. The bench seats were stoutly built out of wood but had cushions tied to them. The cushions were removed periodically so that the covers could be washed clean of the soot and dirt that unavoidably accumulated.

The Third Class carriage was built on the same frame and had a similar overall layout. The seats were made of slatted wooden benches, like those still to be found in parks around the country, and the windows were often open and unglazed.

The First Class carriages at this date were again built on the same chassis, but were much more luxurious. Not only did they have padded and individual seats in place of benches, but each compartment had its own lamp. The wood and paintwork were of a higher quality as were the door handles and other fittings and fixtures.

Camberley station in about 1890. The station was only about 10 years old at this date and drew much of its business from the large military camps and firing ranges that lay in the area.

By 1900 the importance of passenger, and in particular of commuter, traffic had become obvious. The railway companies were making major efforts to improve their carriages. By this date most passenger carriages were mounted on bogies, with four wheels each at either end, and were around 48 feet long. The bogies were equipped with powerful springs that provided suspension, suppressing out the bumps and jinks of the rails for the first time. It was usual for there to be six compartments of seating in each class of carriage, still with seats running the width of the carriage with a door at either side.

First Class carriages were still being designed with an eye on the level of comfort found in private carriages and, increasingly, private motor vehicles. The seats were fitted with deeply sprung bodies topped by a cushion that could be removed for cleaning. The backs of the seats likewise had a cushion. Each seat came with arms and wings, all padded and trimmed. By this date most rail companies had adopted a pattern for their upholstery as well as a standardised paint scheme for their locomotives and rolling stock. The SER, for instance, had a dark blue floral pattern of cloth for its upholstery. The carriage interiors were trimmed with veneers of expensive woods such as maple or walnut.

By this date the comfort of Third Class passengers was being taken rather more seriously. The carriages were still aimed at workmen travelling in their work clothes, but the bare wooden seating had now gone. In its place was cheaper upholstery that could be easily removed for cleaning, together with signs asking passengers not to put dirty boots on to seats.

Second Class was increasingly being squeezed out. The comfort levels were not very much higher than Third Class, but the prices were. Increasingly passengers were choosing to travel either in First Class or Third Class. The numbers of Second Class carriages was first cut back and then dispensed with altogether. By around 1930 no more Second Class carriages were being built. This left the railways with the anomaly of running trains with First Class and Third Class, but no Second Class carriages. The carriages continued to be used on routes running between ports and major cities so that foreigners who had purchased Second Class tickets had Second Class compartments in which to sit. Finally in post-nationalisation days British Rail reallocated its Third Class carriages to be Second Class, then as standard carriages.

By the 1890s most rail companies were offering a range of comforts to their passengers. There were sleeper carriages for overnight, long-distance journeys. There were dining cars for long journeys during the daytime. At first these merely served up dishes prepared at stations but by 1900 there were galleys attached to most dining cars. Toilets were installed early on, but they were generally reserved only for long distances and did not often feature on commuter trains running in Surrey.

It was with this mix of carriages that the rail companies faced up to the challenge of mass commuting in the years after the Great War of 1914-1918.

Chapter 6

The Great Wars

The British Army has always been very interested in Surrey. Its position immediately south of London put it on the direct route of any invading army wanting to land on the South Coast before marching inland to capture London. In 1066 Duke William of Normandy came through Surrey after winning the Battle of Hastings. No English government since has ever wanted an invader to repeat that success, and so far none has.

That does not mean that nobody has planned such a move. In 1804 Emperor Napoleon of France was planning to land at Dover, Folkestone and Hastings before marching inland. He planned to take his main force up the Dover Road to London, but a strong corps was to hook round through Surrey to cut off London from any support coming from the southwest or west. A broadly similar plan was envisaged by Hitler in 1940, though his plan relied more on fast-moving forces of panzers and armoured cars sweeping around London by way of Surrey and Berkshire.

The LB&SCR K Class locomotive No.337. This class of locomotive entered service just in time for the First World War and was to remain active on the Surrey railways through to the 1960s.

Wounded soldiers brought back from France being unloaded from a train at Waterloo Station in the autumn of 1914. Many of these hospital trains ran through Surrey to London, and thousands of the wounded were taken by rail to hospitals in Surrey for treatment and convalescence. Redhill proved to be the busiest junction for these trains, as it was again in 1940.

For centuries the English and then the British governments relied on the navy to stop any invading army from ever landing. In the 1850s, however, strategists began to worry that the navy was no longer able to perform this task. The Commander in Chief of the army, Lord Hardinge, began planning how the army could defend London. He fixed on the towering escarpment of the North Downs as being the best place to stop an invading army. Military engineers were sent out to identify the best places for artillery bastions, infantry trenches and cavalry counter-attacks. Detailed plans were drawn up, but no work was actually done. The areas identified were prime agricultural land that would have been hugely expensive for the army to buy. In any case, Hardinge calculated, the army would have several weeks notice of an invasion given the need for an enemy to declare war, defeat the Royal Navy and get an army over the Channel. There would be plenty of time for his troops to move in and construct the defensive works.

The RAF section of the Whyteleafe cemetery. The majority of the men and women buried here died while serving at the nearby base of RAF Kenley, many of them killed by

German bombing raids. The majority of personnel and supplies for RAF Kenley arrived by rail on the Caterham branch line.

What he needed, in fact, was a place where his troops could be based and trained ready for their task. His eye fell on Farnham and the extensive heaths north of the town. The heath was cheap to buy, while the area was linked to the North Downs by the recently constructed railways. Thus it was that the British army bought up huge areas of open land around the Surrey town of Farnham and the Hampshire town of Aldershot. The massive increase in passenger and freight traffic coming to Farnham led the LSWR to open a new station at Aldershot in 1870 and the SER to open North Camp in 1856. The latter had one of the largest refreshment rooms of any station in England where the soldiers coming on and off duty could slake their thirsts.

A decade later the heathland around Chobham and Bisley, east of the new army camp, was purchased for use as firing ranges. Some of these were opened up to the public for practice at shooting and remain so to this day. In 1890 a branch line was opened from Brookwood to Bisley for the convenience of civilians and soldiers going to the ranges. The tank engine operating the branch line became known, perhaps mockingly, as the "Bisley Bullet".

At the other end of Surrey, Caterham became the home of the Guards Depot in 1877. At first the military population outnumbered that of the civilians, but as the houses built for commuters multiplied the civilians slowly became the more numerous and by the 1920s the town was losing its martial atmosphere.

A train hauled by locomotive 61233 pauses for water at Walton on Thames in 1948. By this date the railways were suffering from war damage and a chronic lack of repair and maintenance work. The government nationalised the system, but the promised massive investment never materialised.

Issued immediately after the end of World War II this set of instructions for coping with snow, fog and snowstorms was published by E.J. Missenden, General Manager, from the Deepdene Hotel in Dorking. The detailed instructions ran to 24 pages of dense type and took account of the heavy wear and tear that had been suffered by the rail network in Surrey during the war.

As with all railways in Britain, those serving Surrey had been asked by the government to draw up contingency plans for altering timetables to allow for the transport of troops, ammunition and other military supplies in case of war. In August 1914 the plans were put into operation. The first signs that the Surrey residents had of how things were changing came when soldiers appeared on the platforms of all stations and on guard beside bridges and crossings. Fear of German spies and saboteurs was great, though as events would show largely unfounded.

Then the military special trains began to run. In Surrey most of these ran on the lines running east to west. Men, munitions and horses were mustered at the camps around Aldershot, then transported east to the Channel ports to be shipped over to France. For weeks these specials ran day and night, then the traffic slackened off. Detailed timetables had been drawn up many months before the war began that ensured that the correct carriages and wagons were available to move men, horses, guns and ammunition at the precise moment that the army was mustering the regiments on to the platforms. So tightly organised was this massive movement of men and material that once it was put in motion it was virtually impossible to stop. Horse transport wagons were attached to trains so that they would carry the horses of a cavalry regiment from Aldershot one day, unload and then be sent off to pick up an artillery battery in Farnham the next. There was little margin for error and even less for variation. Everything had to run like clockwork.

The same system was in place in Germany and has been blamed by some for the outbreak of the war. Germany mobilised against Russia, but the pre-war planning of the military chiefs had envisaged a war against Russia and France. So strict were the railway plans that the only way to mobilise against Russia was to concurrently move troops to the French border. This alarmed the French and brought them into the conflict, which in turn propelled Belgium to hostilities as a result of which Britain went to war.

The British railways performed magnificently. All regular traffic was halted for a period of five days as the military specials dominated the networks. Thousands of men were carried across Surrey to the Channel Ports, and then taken over the Channel to France and Belgium. It amazed everyone concerned that the entire system worked perfectly and that none of the soldiers was seriously injured. There were the usual tearful scenes at railway stations as men went off to war, leaving behind families and loved ones.

At this date the army marched to war on foot. The regiments marched through their home towns to embark at the stations, and most commanders chose to hold parades led by the regimental band and with colours unfurled. The local civilians turned out in large numbers to wave the men off to war. The parades attracted thousands to line the streets. Everyone knew that many of those leaving would never come back, but the men deserved the finest send off possible. Nobody had any idea of the slaughter that was to follow.

Once the main British army was in France there was a lull. The battles of autumn 1914 led only to stalemate and casualties. In the winter the trains began to run again as the reserves were mobilised and increasingly large quantities of munitions were sent out to France.

Some stations and lines became specialised for military purposes. Kempton Park Race Course, for instance, was converted into a depot for army motor vehicles. Trains on the Shepperton Branch increased greatly in number as a result. Epsom Downs, on the other hand, became a vast training ground for soldiers. The Tattenham Corner branch line was taken over entirely by the

Deepcut Station in 1930. The solid wooden structure seen here was erected by Canadian soldiers posted to the area during World War I. The buildings were demolished during the 1930s.

military and a large number of special military trains ran on the Epsom Downs branch as well. Epsom also saw a large number of medical trains. The huge asylums for the mentally ill just outside the town were taken over by the army and casualties from France railed into Epsom station en route to the hospitals. The "Bisley Bullet" line was extended to Pirbright and Deepcut where new military bases were built.

It very quickly became obvious that Redhill could not cope with the massively increased numbers of trains running through it. The junction had always been busy, but now it was excessively so. New sidings had to be installed and the freight yard enlarged to cope. When peace came the numbers of military trains fell slowly, but dramatically. For some months there were trains bringing the men home, and some continued to take supplies out to the regiments occupying Germany. Eventually the railways returned to peace time running.

In some areas the extra facilities installed to help the military were retained. Redhill, for instance, kept its complex and extensive new layout. Elsewhere the improvements proved to be only temporary. The Bisley extension was lifted in 1921 after the military decided that it did not need it in peacetime. It was to be relaid again, however, when war with Germany came again in 1939. It was but one of many changes that came to the Surrey railway network during World War II.

At first, World War II began much as had World War I so far as the Surrey railways were concerned. There was an initial surge of activity as troops and munitions were shipped west to east across the county from the Aldershot camps to the Channel ports and so to France. Then there followed a lull — longer this time as the "phoney war" stretched from the autumn of 1939 to the spring of 1940 without any serious land fighting. In other ways things were different. The army now travelled largely on motorised transport, so there were few ceremonial parades through towns as the men marched down to the railway stations. And this time everyone feared a repeat of the earlier bloodbath.

In May 1940 the Germans struck, launching a Blitzkrieg campaign that would end at Dunkirk. Now the main traffic was from east to west. Trains carrying thousands of soldiers evacuated from Dunkirk to escape the closing German trap thundered through Surrey. Crowds gathered along the lines to watch the passing trains packed with wounded, exhausted and yet still defiant troops. For seven days all normal trains were suspended.

Once again, Redhill was the busiest junction. In those seven days a total of

A squadron of RAF Hurricane fighters on patrol over Surrey in 1939. These fighters formed the backbone of the aerial defences of Surrey when war broke out. The more glamorous Spitfires were then available only in limited numbers.

565 evacuation specials passed through the station, causing the railways companies to suspend all civilian trains. It was not only that men needed to be moved. They also had to be cared for. Temporary kitchens were set up at stations where tea could be brewed up and vast pots of soup or stew set to boil. As soon as a train pulled in teams of railway workers would pour on board armed with mugs of tea or soup to hand out to the exhausted, famished soldiers. Nor were the emotional needs of the soldiers forgotten. Each man was given a postcard on which was pre-printed a message saying that the man had been safely evacuated from France and was being taken to barracks in England to recover. There was a space for the man to write his name and another for him to write the name and address of the relative to whom the card was to be sent. The cards were handed out at one station, then collected at the next and posted.

Unsurprisingly the railway staff at most stations could not cope with the tasks given them. Stationmasters everywhere asked for volunteers from the local community to help hand out tea or postcards. Most young people were at work, so in most places it was elderly women who responded to the call.

Everyone knew Dunkirk had been a defeat of great scale, and they knew also that a German invasion was likely within weeks.

No sooner had the evacuation stopped than the troops were back. This time they were converting railway embankments into hurriedly constructed fortresses complete with machine gun nests, pill boxes and tank traps. Cuttings were similarly converted, and bridges were prepared for demolition to try to slow down advancing German panzers. And while all this work went on, new military specials thundered over the lines carrying ammunition and spare parts to the bases of RAF Fighter Command to enable them to fight the Battle of Britain. One of the busiest stations in Surrey during this time was Whyteleafe, which served the RAF fighter base at nearby Kenley.

The Germans recognised the importance of the Surrey railways, so the Luftwaffe came in to bomb them. Sunbury Station was destroyed and the lines leading to Hampton Court knocked out. Tattenham Corner station was bombed, and though the station buildings escaped the sidings and rail lines were smashed. The nearby Epsom Downs line was severed for several days by bomb damage. An attempt to bomb the vulnerable Drift Bridge on the Epsom Downs line resulted only in the destruction of a few nearby houses. The author is currently writing this book in a studio erected on that bomb site.

The most dramatic incident came on 16 December 1942 when a Dornier Do217 attacked a train running from Guildford to Horsham. The German plane opened fire with its machine guns as it came down very low, then it dropped a bomb beside the line that exploded on the earthen bank of the cutting just north of Bramley through which the train was running. A total of seven people were killed and over 50 injured. The casualties might have been worse, but a formation of Canadian troops saw the attack and ran to help, administering prompt battlefield first aid to the severely injured and so saving many lives.

It was not, however, the bombing that did the most damage to the railways of Surrey. The huge workload placed on track, buildings, locomotives and rolling stock was immense. Given the pressures of war time, many routine repairs and maintenance were overlooked. Rolling stock was worked beyond the limits of endurance, tracks were overloaded and points allowed to deteriorate.

Among the most effective locomotives used during both world wars was the LB&SCR K Class. Their design and history will serve to illustrate how carefully the railways operating over Surrey designed and maintained their locomotives.

The LB&SCR had very special requirements of its freight engines due to the fact that most of its profit came from passenger trains. The freight trains were required to keep out of the way, meaning that they had to be able to accelerate quickly from sidings and signals, and then keep up a good speed to their destination. Above all they had to be reliable and not be subject to breakdowns.

In 1913 a new type of modern freight locomotives was ordered from the company's Brighton Works. The resulting "K" class were 2-6-0 locomotives equipped with a Belpaire firebox, Robinson-style superheaters and two large inclined outside cylinders with Stephenson valve gear. The boilers were fed by hot water injectors, operated by a Weir pump, and surplus steam fed back to the tenders to preheat the water. The tenders were the largest of any LB&SCR locomotive with a capacity of 3940 gallons of water and 4 tons of coal.

The first two K class locomotives entered service in September and December 1913, and three more followed in the spring of 1914. These five locomotives did sterling work during the First World War. They were capable of hauling trains of up to 1,000 tons at 35 mph, for long distances. They also withstood the punishing schedule of frequent runs and infrequent servicing better than most other models. As a result five more were constructed for 1916 and ten more were ordered as soon as the war ended.

The K Class spent the interwar years working on freight and, sometimes, passenger duties on the lines around Surrey and Sussex. When the Second World War came the K class were once more pressed into military service. Once again they hauled heavy loads with ease and reliability, and saw their busiest time in the run up to D-Day in 1944.

After the war the robust locomotives were found to be in good working order and so were heavily used while other locomotives were refurbished or new vehicles bought in. As demand for freight trains fell, the K class found themselves underused, though some were put on to passenger services. In November and December 1962 all the K Class locomotives were withdrawn from service. There was nothing wrong with them even then, almost 50 years after they were built. They were retired as part of a wider programme to abandon steam in favour of diesel and electric locomotives. They were all broken up.

By the time peace came in 1945 the railways were in serious need of massive repairs, refurbishment and modernisation. They had played their role in gaining victory and had suffered accordingly. They needed a fortune spending on them. Sadly the post-war government had other priorities. The railways were nationalised, but the promised government spending never materialised.

The railways were on a downward path of decline. It was the end of an era.

Chapter 7

The End of an Era

The coming of the steam railways wrought many changes to Surrey. What had been a rural county — albeit one heavily influenced by proximity to London — was rapidly transformed into a county where rural pursuits were very much in a minority. Towns grew rapidly, suburbs for commuters sprang up just as quickly and increasingly the county was dependent on the capital city.

Yet, the age of steam could not last. Steam power had driven the industrial revolution and transformed transport networks beyond imagining. Steam did, however, have its drawbacks. Steam engines took a lot of looking after. They had to be fired up before they could be used so that steam pressure could build up in the boiler. They had to be cleaned regularly, not only on the exterior

A GWR diesel locomotive trundles through Staines. The Great Western Railway never adopted electrification so as the steam age came to a close it re-equipped with diesel locomotives.

Competition from road transport is often blamed for the closure of rural railways, but in some areas buses were essential for trav-ellers wanting to get from the rail station to their final destination. This Route No.79 is waiting at Uckfield in 1923.

where soot and grime collected but also inside the boilers where lithe men were sent with wire brushes to scrape and scrub the piping clean to keep the boilers efficient. When on the rails, the steam trains could be slow to get moving out of a station. On commuter lines where passenger trains might start and stop again every three or four miles this was more of a problem than on long distance lines between major cities.

Travellers complained in summer that if they kept the carriage windows closed they stifled in the heat, but if they opened them soot and grime would blow in. More than one commuter had a wife who complained about black grime on shirt collars and cuffs. Moreover the housebuilders who were increasingly providing the Surrey railway companies with their income via commuters found that they faced a problem. People wanted to live within easy walking distance of the station, but nobody wanted to be so close to the line that washing hung out to dry got covered in soot.

These various factors convinced the various railways companies that they should seek to find an alternative to steam traction on the commuter routes.

First into the fray was the London & Brighton Electric Railway which sponsored a Bill in Parliament in 1901. This new company wanted to build a monorail system, promising to reduce journey times from London to Brighton to 40 minutes. The LB&SCR responded by starting to run a London-Brighton express service that covered the distance in just 51 minutes. That was enough to make the provision of a new electric link uneconomic and the idea died.

Competition on other routes was more determined. In northeastern Surrey many of the new commuter housing estates were being linked into the electric tram network. This method of getting to work was not as speedy as the trains, but it was cleaner and more convenient. The LB&SCR in particular began to lose income to the trams and in 1912 the board of directors decided to invest in electrification of 47 miles of track as an experiment.

The system chosen by the LB&SCR was an overhead electrical system. This meant that the trains were powered by electricity conducted through cables strung over the rail lines. The engines had sprung pick ups pushed up from their roofs which collected the electricity and conducted it down to the motors. The system was known colloquially in the LB&SCR as "The Overheads". At first the system seemed to be doing well. In 1909 a short stretch from Battersea Park to East Brixton stations in south London was opened. That was successful so the go ahead was given to convert the rest of the 47 miles of experimental track.

One of the very few railway stations in Surrey to fail to have survived to the present day is Bramley and Wonersh, seen here in about 1908. With the exception of the *wooden-framed signal box all the buildings are still standing and today form part of an industrial estate.*

Unfortunately the LB&SCR had chosen to purchase all their equipment from Allgemeine Elektricitats Gesselschaft (AEG) of Berlin. When World War I broke out the supply of equipment and spares ceased at once and electrification came to a halt. It was not until 1922 that work began again, but by then major changes were underway. The assorted railway companies that served Surrey were in 1923 amalgamated to form the Southern Railways (SR). The move was forced on the railways by the government which felt that a more strategic approach to rail transportation was needed than could be achieved by the existing companies. The board of SR very quickly opted to standardise on the LSWR system of having a third rail to carry the electricity. The "Overheads" were doomed.

The SR chose to advertise their newly electrified commuter lines under the title of "Southern Electrics", producing a mass of advertising and promotional material. The first section of Southern Electric commuter trains began operation on 12 July 1925 running from Raynes Park to Dorking via Epsom. The stretches of line from Leatherhead to Guildford and Surbiton to Effingham

East Croydon Station in about 1910. The electric trams that are evident in this picture were at this time posing a real threat to the railway companies as they were attracting many of the commuters off the trains.

An early Southern Electric train at Tattenham Corner. The line to this station was electrified on the third rail system in June 1928, though steam trains continued to work the line for freight and race day specials for many years afterward.

Junction began operation later the same day. Thereafter electrification proceeded rapidly. By 1929 the first phase of electrification was completed and all the main commuter routes were operating trains powered by Electrical Multiple Units (EMUs). In 1931 the main lines to Brighton, Portsmouth and Eastbourne were electrified. For the rest of the 1930s electrification continued at a slower pace, investment being hard to come by in the economic depression of the 1930s. Despite this work, the Southern Railway continued to operate steam locomotives on long distance routes, for freight trains and for various shunting work.

The electrification of the commuter lines led to a second burst of house building in many towns across Surrey. Much of this new construction was of houses considerably smaller and cheaper than those built before. Commuting was now a popular lifestyle choice for many in middle ranks of management and skilled manual workers. Ashtead, for instance, saw a rapid development of greenfield sites around the station. Its population had already increased from 926 in 1881 to 3,226 in 1921. By 1939 the population had boomed again to 9,300. The pattern was matched elsewhere. Claygate increased in population from 2,860 in 1921 to 6,900.

Some places were born as entirely new communities between the wars as electrification boosted the numbers of people wanting to commute. The line between Surbiton and Claygate passed through open countryside until 1930 when a new station was built on farmland and named Hinchley Wood after a nearby stand of trees. Property developers laid out a form of village green lined by shops just outside the station, with hundreds of houses being built over the nearby fields. The house adverts proudly proclaimed that the housing estate had its own Southern Electric station. The houses were rapidly snapped

An electric train pulls into Warlingham in the 1970s. These slam-door electric trains were ubiquitous on the rail network in Surrey at this time.

up. Hersham was another station constructed at this time in collaboration with house builders who recognised that the presence of a Southern Electric station was essential to the financial success of their constructions.

When World War II ended in 1945 Surrey had a rather run down railway infrastructure. The electric lines continued to carry thousands of commuters into London every day, while steam locomotives hauled freight, mail and long distance trains. The only tracks that were not electrified was the Oxted to East Grinstead line in the east of the county. The SR had intended to electrify this line in 1940, but the war had stopped the work from taking place. It is symptomatic of the lack of investment that blighted the nationalised railways after the war that the line was still operated under steam in 1963. This line was the last in Surrey to see steam locomotives in operation. On 6 January 1964 the route was taken over by diesel locomotives. It was finally electrified in 1987.

The age of steam in Surrey was over.

Bretwalda Books Ltd

Bretwalda Books has a website on
www.BretwaldaBooks.com

Bretwalda Books runs a blog on
http://bretwaldabooks.blogspot.com/

Bretwalda Books is on FaceBook as
Bretwalda Books

Bretwalda Books is on Twitter as
Bretwaldabooks

Bretwalda Books has a channel on Youtube as
BretwaldaBooks

The author of this book, Rupert Matthews, has a website on
www.rupertmatthews.com